*To Mark*

# Becoming
# Unique

*Best Wishes*
*J. Charles*

*James Charles*

**Clink
Street**

London | New York

Published by Clink Street Publishing 2015

Copyright © James Charles 2015

First edition.

ISBN: 978-1-909477-90-2
Ebook: 978-1-909477-91-9

This book is dedicated to the many silent voices of Autism, as well as the countless unpaid and forgotten carers. This book is also dedicated to the many been bullied, threatened and abused due to disability, religion, race, nationality, opinions and sexual orientation. While remembering these many victims, let's not forget many, who fought against bigotry, discrimination and against the many injustices throughout history. At this stage I would like to remember lost family members and friends who made valuable contributions to my self-worth. I would like to thank my wife Helen for her ongoing support. Thanks to my parents, the Cattell family, brothers, sisters, nieces, nephews, inlaws and extended family of cousins, aunts and uncles. I would also like to thank Michael Bermingham, Devi Kularatne and Ann Hill, as well as the book publishers.

# Contents

# Book Writing

*"Creativity comes in many forms; we see it mostly in artists, musicians, poets and writers. As a music lover I have seen many greats making cover versions their own, for it has been said Shakespeare made many existing plays his own. Even today we see photographs of particular locations as just another photo, while another photo of the same location may become a masterpiece. Creativity can be shown in people's taste of music or taste in literature. Even within those books people's individuality and creativity can be shown in what they underline, as they read."*
( Myself, 2014)

Book writing was something I always wanted to do; after all, as a teenager I had a strong desire to be a journalist. Although some of the books I thought about writing then, I can certainly say now I'm glad I never got started on, never mind got published. Yet as my teens progressed I learnt of the great Irish contribution to English literature, for instance, Yeats, Wilde, O'Casey, Joyce and Behan – and the list could go on. However, living in the literature world came to an end on entering the working world, where creative thinking and problem solving served no purpose in many jobs. Saying that, I still would love to work as a journalist, as I remember when growing up in

Ireland I wanted to expose the exploitations of the money lenders, but writing now there's many more truths I wish to see exposed and I still feel very strongly about the ethics of journalists and the battles they face with the owners of the media.

There are many journalists I have admired over the years, who include John Pilger, Fintan O'Toole, Paul Foot and the many journalists who worked for newspapers like *The Guardian*, *The Independent* and *New Statesman*. While I was growing up in County Leitrim, Ireland, there were two particular journalists that inspired me who wrote for the *Longford News* and the *Leitrim Observer*. Sadly I cannot remember their names, but then it is my inability to remember that has contributed to my struggles in education over the years. Yet over forty years ago education and learning gave me a great dislike of book reading and attending school.

Attending school became a different experience for me when I started attending school in Ireland. Despite that, my parents worked hard to teach us to read and the teachers did play their role well. My interest in reading was helped by my love for history especially, and writing now I think it is very important to explore children's interest, as an encouragement for those having reading difficulties. In my school days there was often little consideration for kids who may have had mental health issues, dyslexia or autism. Having struggled to learn to read, the next demon was spelling, which led to much caning in school. My hatred for spelling was overtaken by hatred for poetry, so it will surprise many that I have included some of my poetry in this book. It was often asked, what use is poetry when entering the work world? The answer to that question is "I don't know", but I do feel if some people working on the buildings learned more history, there would be better regard for old historic buildings. While school may not have been for everyone, subjects like history have even been questioned by certain historians, who say "history is told by winners".

Becoming an historian and rewriting history was not an option for me, when leaving school with a struggling leaving cert. Yet many pupils completing their leaving cert were inspired to write by the story of Peig Sayers, which was part of the Irish leaving cert syllabus. Peig Sayers was a woman from County Kerry in Ireland who lived through hard times in the late nineteenth and early twentieth centuries. What's interesting is that the story of Peig Sayers is told by word of mouth and, I was to later learn, there were many more books relayed by illiterate people. By my late teens I had developed an interest in poetry as I was inspired by the punk poet John Cooper Clarke. I had also realized that poetry was the backbone of some of the greatest songs ever written. However, this sense of cultural awareness was irrelevant when moving to England in 1986.

By the end of 1986 I was working in unskilled manual work in Luton. At times I felt no different from my parents' generation, who had emigrated to England with only a primary school education. However, by the end of 1987 I was a part-time student, I had left Luton and I was starting to meet more like minded people. My hopes to become a writer were given a boost when I was complimented on my report writing ability. It was around this time I started writing poetry. My first poem, "This World", was written as a means to ventilate many of my frustrations. Later some of my poems would be collaborated into songs with some friends, but my desire was to write a novel.

The first novel I attempted to write was about a young Irish poet who moves to London, with the hopes of becoming a rock star. The book starts with the young man starting off his first band in Ireland and the band making the first gig at a local charity concert. Sadly the band breaks up after a few months, following many disagreements. The book looks at the young man making an impact in London and experiencing a great homecoming gig. Part of the book was based on my wish to be in music and live a cosmopolitan lifestyle in London, but I found the experience of writing the book a drag. The story continues with the young man falling in love, but that soon ends and he commits suicide. This was the late 1980s and I felt I lacked the imagination to write a novel.

About the same time a friend of mine who had read some of my poetry suggested I write a book about my arrival in England. When starting writing it I felt that sharing the fact I had failed many job interviews and got sacked from a number of jobs would be a family embarrassment. Another fact had to be admitted: to being educated later than many and having to lie about my age. While many mature students were happy to talk about quitting education due to lack of interest or wanting greater adventure, this was not the case for me. I was a mature student because I was too "fucking" thick and over the years my many battles with work management would be due to incompetencies. Yet in my line of work as a teaching assistant many kids will brag about failing maths, but difficulty in reading can still be a taboo and a silent embarrassment for many. As was my own difficulty in education in the early 1990s.

The early 1990s was a time my heart was broken by love and the terrible state of the world gave me much ammunition to write poetry. Around the same time I was writing my agony of love journals, with the hope of turning them into a novel. Despite disguising names and places, I decided to abandon the project. I also felt it brought up too many painful recordings, as well as exposing certain individuals. As the 1990s progressed I changed location many times, which meant losing not only much music, books and other belongings, but also my writing material. However, some of the recorded and ventilated painful memories were something that perhaps needed to go. Although losing my poetry collection was a loss as I had hopes of putting all my poetry together in one book.

By the late 1990s I was living more in the real world deciding on a career in nursing. A career in nursing would provide the opportunity to be in a stable employment, as well as the opportunity to experience working holidays around the world. As a then revolutionary I felt as a mental health nurse I would be needed following the revolution. Being both a revolutionary and a student I was always keen to do literature searches on topics of interest. The twentieth century was closing, but the same could not be said for emerging scandals in Irish history. I felt the desire to do some historic research with the aim of writing a book called *"Unmasking the Faces of Irish History"*. Sadly this project would have to wait until I finished my nursing studies, by which time I had become a mental health nurse and I was also becoming more of a lapsed socialist.

In the early part of the twenty-first century, I struggled as a mental health nurse. It was also around that time I rediscovered my Catholic faith. I feel it was my faith and belief in God or something of a higher being that got me through many difficult times in nursing. Prior to moving to Horsefield in 2008 to further my career opportunities, I observed how my faith had taken a turnaround in less than ten years, and I considered writing "Journey of Faith".

"Journey of Faith" would eventually become part of this book, *Becoming Unique*. Unfortunately moving to

Horsefield meant writing would be put on hold, as I was starting to doubt my faith. Soon I would be having doubts about my ability to communicate and to be a nurse. Yet my time in Horsefield was when I would discover something very important about myself – I had Autistic Spectrum Disorder (ASD).

My self discovery of having ASD was a great relief and it was round this time my wife suggested I write a book. At first I was unsure, but I soon warmed to the idea when my contract at Horsefield was coming to an end. It was round this time I started writing drafts for this book, but it was often difficult as emotions were high because Horsefield posed certain challenges in my life (which having ASD would do when I returned to the West Midlands, especially when looking for work). This compelled me to open up about the many struggles I had experienced in my younger years. I felt I had to bare all in order to be understood. This was the end of 2013 and I started to study to be a life coach and expand my training into Complementary Therapies.

Time was spent as book writing took many hours over the weeks and months; time was also needed for going through what was written and changing certain details. As well as those tasks, time was also spent protecting the dignity of many individuals. This poses the question "where was the free time?" Well, the way I look at it, when I first moved to England in 1986 I was working in two jobs for almost seventy hours a week and little pay. That's not including travel time and time to prepare, with little free time. While in more recent years I remember having to book a week's annual leave to complete my nursing mentorship course. So the way I looked at it, if I spent all those hours over the years working for others, "why not spend the hours working on something useful for myself?"

# Autistic Struggles

As a young care worker in my early twenties I remember observing a man, possibly in his thirties, having a severe temper tantrum. I thought, it's difficult for parents having to deal with young children with temper tantrums, but imagine dealing with similar temper tantrums exhibited by grown men. I later learnt not only had this man severe learning disabilities but he was also autistic, and quite a high percentage of people who are autistic also have a severe learning disability. It would still be a number of years till I discovered I was autistic myself and I have learnt that much anger and violence are a result of misunderstood frustrations. There are many areas of autism still misunderstood even by professionals and even though I was a mental health nurse for ten years I still have difficulty ventilating my frustrations on occasions. Awareness of autism, I feel, is important, but as I have said to certain people, "if you think I am easy to restrain, imagine dealing with someone twice my size with little anger control and twice my fitness". While increasing amounts of literature has now been written on autism, I found only a little useful information when I became aware of being autistic in my forties. Yet despite that I have learnt to overcome some of my own frustrations and share where it all began.

To start, I was born in The Foresters Arms in Luton, England on December 26th 1965. My parents, Vincent Charles and Kathleen (nee McIntyre), both came from Aughavas, County Leitrim in Ireland. Luton had such a big Irish community, especially from County Leitrim; I could consider myself Leitrim born. Less than a year old, we moved to London where my father ran the pub The Neptune near Mornington Crescent. It was here my sister Maria and brother VG were born and it was here my earliest memories are from. By 1969 the family had moved back to Luton, where my brother Nigel was born, and by 1971 I had started attending primary school at St Margaret's, Farley Hill, in Luton. I really enjoyed school there and seemed to get on well with most of the kids and I remember having one particular black friend. It's difficult to remember how successful academically I was then, but writing now I remember forgetting messages. Overall, memories seemed to be happy, as there was the nuclear family and the extended family, as well as family friends, who were mainly Irish. However, this was to change when we moved to Ireland in December 1971; although I was not anticipating this move with fear, as I had spent some time in Ireland a year previously.

As on many occasions throughout my life I formed expectations and many were unrealistic. For while I enjoyed staying with the grannies, I expected we would move to Dublin and not settle in rural Ireland. It was round this time Bloody Sunday in Derry took place and there was much anger towards Britain in Ireland. The British Embassy in Dublin was burned, and there were many examples of anti British feelings. Still, this was unknown to me and when I started school in Rossan, Aughavas in County Leitrim, I received physical and verbal abuse for being English (or alleged English). Saying that, I feel a similar fate may have awaited me if I had been Irish born moving to a school in England.

Back then it was a culture shock for me having attended a school in England then moving to a small school in Ireland, where I seem to remember kids were no longer wearing school uniforms, but some were wearing dirty clothes and Wellington boots? Looking back, then many would have envied living somewhere free from pop culture. While rural Ireland was not like England, almost every house did have a television and names like David Cassidy were not unknown.

The house where my parents still live had no electricity or no running water when we first moved in and I soon became a school dunce. The school itself had no flush toilets and that's where I learned not to have a shit in the day time, perhaps a reason that explains constipation throughout my life. While the other family members seemed to settle in well, I found rural Ireland a culture shock, as well as taking the abuse at school very personally, which seemed to affect much of my self-esteem throughout my life. Perhaps one of the reasons was that much of rural Ireland never saw the 1960s and even in the 1970s, Ireland never saw the Western sexual revolution or easing of corporal punishment in schools. When I started Rossan school in 1972 Eamon De Valera was still president of Ireland and the Catholic Church ruled with an iron fist.

For me these were difficult changes, even looking back now, with school dinners replaced by horrible sandwiches and the education system different. I had also lost all my school friends in England and I was missing my aunts, uncles and cousins who had remained in England. It became further confusing when my mother had to go to hospital for some time when expecting the fifth member of the family and now having granny around affected my routine. Unknown to me at the time, routine was very important as it prevented much anxiety. While I loved my grannies, I could not bear home without my mother. Yet after my mother gave birth to my sister Antoinette, I have few further memories other than preparation for First Holy Communion.

I had little interest in sport but in 1974 I started watching the World Cup, having discovered the rules of Association Football (soccer as I called it) easy to follow. Despite this lack of interest I had enjoyed watching cricket on television when I was in England, prior to the family returning to Ireland. Football became part of school break-time routine until I moved to secondary school, as before that I had difficulty mixing with others and joining in games. Break-time memories seem to consist of often being kept in for falling behind in my lessons and I seemed to be kept in with those Mr Donavan thought would be hopeless cases in the future. However, I think it was a surprise to Mr Donavan that I attended university in later years.

Perhaps the most prominent memory is of being caned, often for offences I can't remember but more often for not getting my maths or spelling right, especially Irish spelling. I hated "fucking" Irish and I think the way it was forced on us made many unable to speak the language today. Having to recite poetry was another frightening experience as I could never remember my lines and it scared me away from stage acting in later years, in case I forgot my lines. As I write other memories arise, like being made to stand up in front of the classroom and being laughed at by kids. The fact is I tried hard to learn but nothing was going into my thick brain and I was living in fear of being caned. Around that time I remember saying to one of the family, "if I was teaching I would not use the cane". I felt I was looked upon as a sissy for suggesting such a soft approach idea. Yet I am proud to say I was able to use a more humane approach in my teaching role in later years. However, back in the 1970s, I remember my bad temper being a concern among my family, and even now I can record memories of feeling frustrated.

The caning continued in 1975 and it was a difficult time for me, as my mother was once again in hospital and granny was managing the house. At this stage I think I was becoming withdrawn into myself, as I remember identifying with a boy in a French film in which at the end he goes happily up into the air with his balloon collection. School was even more miserable and caning for not getting spellings right became regular practice. One day it hit breaking point when Mr Donavan asked me to put out my hand for more slaps. I refused and in anger tried to pull the stick from him. It was futile and I ended up getting further beatings, and to add to that I was just seen as stupid by the rest of the pupils. For years I felt angry about how I was treated, but now I regret my actions and I would like to apologize to Mr Donavan before it's too late. I now feel many schools were not equipped to deal with kids with autism, nor other learning needs.

Forgetfulness often played a role when attending school. I remember on one occasion leaving my copy book at school and because of that I felt unable to do my homework. When I explained this to Mr Donavan he sarcastically said "is there paper at home?" and he then caned me. I felt unjustly punished but once, many years later, when shopping I was unable to buy certain items due to their non availability. This seemed no excuse to my wife, who was angry I had not bought some substitute items and then made a few out of order comments. I decided to withdraw to another room in the house, as angry thoughts were going through my head and I was having flashbacks of memories from my school days. I started feeling sorry for myself, that my wife often misunderstood me like teachers and people in the past. Unlike Mr Donavan, my wife has had to tolerate my criticisms and certain intolerances, as well as my lack of flexibility. Yet talking about my school days as if they were yesterday is often due to recent events that bring back memories as vivid as today.

Growing up in Ireland in the 1970s was stressful, especially when I was seen as the most disastrous pupil in Rossan School. In many ways I was seen as strange, but I looked down my nose on those who had offensive odour and those with little general knowledge or culture. Indeed, my attitude was similar when I felt certain nurses lacked general knowledge and culture more than twenty years later. Back in the 1970s I was sometimes blunt in my comments and yet I often expected people to behave in a certain manner. I remember my younger brother asking my granny why she could not have babies and granny said she was too old; I then explained to my brother she could not have babies because she was a widow. My "should be" expectations also meant I was not impressed with kids who wanted to fight.

I hated fighting and this happened in many schools, but many of these kids grew up and did well despite low expectations. While fighting was direct aggression, at least you often knew where you stood. For in later years I would encounter indirect aggression, which I would compare to unknown viruses building up in someone's computer over many years. Looking back, Rossan School and Aughavas produced a good generation of people and many I am now in contact with through my social networks. Reflecting now, growing up in Ireland carved out much of my identity. Much of that time I wished my family would move back to England, but I had interests like football to keep me motivated.

During the 1970s I was a Liverpool football supporter and I looked forward to Saturday and the football results. Been a Liverpool football supporter kept me different from those who supported Manchester United. Yet when it came to football in Scotland we were all united in cheering for Glasgow Celtic. I was less keen on Gaelic football as I found it more difficult to play; I also was not keen on the attitude of some, calling soccer an English man's game and a woman's sport. Despite that I went to watch our local Gaelic Football team, Aughavas, play almost every Sunday. Gaelic, soccer and Rugby were well liked among my brothers and me, but also liked by many at school. Association Football was so much liked in our family that one of my brothers had a desire to be a professional footballer. My brother said to one of the neighbours, "I don't need to be good at my books, because I am going to be a professional soccer player". When the neighbour said she would go and see him play when he was grown up my brother replied:

"Ah no, Mrs K..., you will be long dead".

I too had a desire to be a professional footballer in England, even though I was one of the slowest runners in Leitrim. If Association Football or soccer was one of my escapes then the other was fetching water from the well in the evenings, where I would have time to myself and nature. My love for nature also extended to the love for my cats, but I was made aware that only girls and sissy boys liked cats.

School was a struggle, yet I discovered one subject that motivated me was history, which I think motivated me to stay on in school. Even when I was aged ten I use to enjoy watching history programmes on television. Actually I used to prefer non-fiction to fiction and in many ways little has changed. My historical hero was Daniel O'Connell and I was fascinated by how he fought for Catholic Emancipation and believed in freedom for Ireland by peaceful means. This was when the Troubles in Northern Ireland were at their peak, but writing now I think many Tory Catholic MPs in Westminster today should be thankful to Daniel O'Connell for paving the way for Catholics to enter Westminster. My interest in history helped in my interest in politics and as a young boy I was known for my awareness of the world political leaders. I remember being an admirer of the American President Jimmy Carter and writing now, almost forty years later, I make no apologies. Jimmy Carter represented the Liberal and Democratic politics, as well as the equality and fair play that I admired.

While primary school provided many negative memories, some of my happiest memories were my times off sick from school. My mother really looked out for us when we were ill, as she had a great therapeutic presence in the house. I guess being sick was also a time away from school fears, homework, work around the house, punishments and of freedom from responsibilities. However, for me, "responsibilities" was taking the blame and facing punishments for the consequential outcomes. In many ways I think this fear is still with me now, but it certainly was high on my anxiety agenda for many years. I can honestly say, almost every morning walking to Rossan School I felt fear and anxiety. Fear and anxiety are things no kid should be feeling when going to school, as school is meant to be the best days of our lives. Yet there was little sympathy from older generations, who would tell us how harshly they were punished in their school days. Perhaps my feeling safe when ill equates to why many people can only cope by being in the sick role.

The sick role may have had significance in my school years, but I think that would be liable if most employers said that about me over the last twenty-eight years of working. Yet writing now and being temporarily off work ill, one of my greatest memories was having the measles in winter 1976. Although feeling ill I felt so relieved at not having to go to school and home seemed so peaceful, as my father was away at work and I listened to the radio, hearing the music of Chicago – "If You Leave Me Now" – and the ELO. RTE radio also introduced me to radio drama and radio documentaries, which is perhaps why I now like BBC Radio 4 and audio books. In 1976 I was not exactly into the punk scene, which by the late 1970s had become a half trend in itself. I do remember liking Eddie and the Hot Rods, who were more Rock 'n' Roll to me. Actually punk music to me sounded more like T-Rex, and while I was not highly music cultured, this was no crime where I grew up, as young people in their twenties seemed to follow Country and Show-band music.

I remember the Christmas of 1976 in particular as it was when perhaps the greatest Christmas song was released – Chris De Burg, "Spaceman Came Travelling". Shame about his other records. I also remember that Christmas coming to an end and saying to my mother, "I wish it could be Christmas every day" and my mum saying, "You would get fed up of Christmas". That made sense to me and was to be one of my many learning experiences in life, as over the years, and even now, I am amazed at what does not come natural to me. I think much of my cognitive development and learning took place in the 1970s.

Yet my cognitive development seemed too slow for my teacher, as I was kept back a year. For me this was a humiliation, being the oldest and the dunce of the class, as well as having to bear another year in primary school. Looking back, I might have done no worse in secondary school if I had started in 1978.

I remember the 1970s being classed as the boring decade, unlike the 1960s, although it was often a Conservative version presented. Yet I did not admire the Far Right politics and I remember in the 1970s Fine Gael being nicknamed "The Blueshirts". The Blueshirts were a Fascist group led by Eoin O'Duffy in the 1930s and were part of the dark Irish Far Right political history. Eoin O'Duffy eventually founded Fine Gael and there was an athletic competition named the "O'Duffy Cup". Athletics was something we were all apart of when attending Rossan School, but athletics was not my strong point. I remember deciding that if I were selected for the O'Duffy Cup, I would not compete as O'Duffy was a Blueshirt and a Fascist.

On a positive note, the 1970s was a decade for many albums – artists like Pink Floyd, Yes, Horslips, The Eagles, Neil Young and Van Morrison. I also remember being fascinated by classic album covers when visiting record shops. I guess growing up in County Leitrim meant in the 1970s I never experienced the youth culture of that time and what it was like to be a proper teenager then. Although many people would have not have had the option to experience youth culture with work, and even fewer opportunities to experience the youth and art culture; many of those who were punks were often art students. For me, I had enough interests, like sport, history, politics, and classical architecture, and I was fascinated with modern and future electronic gadgets. However, some of my fascinations and interests would create difficulties in my social interaction skills in later years.

One of my earliest memories of where my fascination and interests overtook everything else was when my mother was going to hospital to have my little sister Grainne in 1979. It was the day RTE launched its first music radio station, RTE radio 2, and as soon as I got home from school, I tuned in to the new radio station. I was so excited, as this was a life changing experience for me, but not for my mother, who was trying to organize herself before going to hospital. From an autistic viewpoint, this would not be the first pre-occupation with my interests that would affect family life. However, at that time RTE radio 2 (now 2fm) opened my world to music, as a then thirteen year old it was often one of my stress escapes. To be honest I never heard much decent new wave music and prior to RTE radio 2, I don't think the Sex Pistols were ever played on radio in 1977. Actually the only way many got to know the Sex Pistols was hearing children singing "Friggin in the Riggin". RTE radio 2 paved a successful route for many upcoming bands over the years, including The Radiators, The Blades and U2. As RTE has been funded by tax payers I think it is disappointing U2 have left Ireland to avoid paying tax, when tax funded radio stations promoted their music.

By 1979 the long wait had come to an end: I was finished with Rossan School and a new, modern secondary school at Moyne was something to look forward to. Moyne was a school local enough for me, as many who were attending Moyne I knew from also attending church at Legga. Secondary school would mean a greater sense of freedom, unlike in primary school where even forgetting to do homework would be a caning offence. It was perhaps my first sense of freedom, with the first experience of having to make decisions for myself. Yet prior to starting secondary school at Moyne, there were many exaggerated stories and much idle gossip circling around about the school. Needless to say much was untrue and it sounded more like the TV drama *Grange Hill* or the banned RTE TV drama *Spike.*

I can't remember what height I was when I started secondary school, but those in the senior years looked more like adults. As for the girls in Secretarial class, they did not wear school uniforms and some looked and dressed more like grown women. Despite many looking like grown-up curvy women, these were still teenage girls in women's bodies. Back then there was little progression from teenager to adulthood and many of these older teenagers were vulnerable to advances from grown men who knew how to use charm. Writing now, it is interesting, in my occasional middle aged teaching role, to observe the vulnerabilities in many teenage children. Going back into childhood memories can be difficult, but teaching and coaching these kids allows me to see my teenage years from outside the box.

In the late 1970s and early 1980s my mother would often talk about feeling sorry for secondary school teachers who have to deal with disruptive teenagers. I would go on to say many of those teachers would have a greater challenge in schools these days. Yet kids are kids and during my experience in teaching and as a church youth leader, most kids have been lovely to work with. Working for many years in learning disabilities and mental health I knew of many kids excluded from school or heard adults in the mental health service talking about their kids' behavioural problems. So I guess working in mainstream education, despite its many challenges, could be a teddy bears' picnic on occasions.

Looking back now, Rossan School sheltered me from my many secondary school embarrassments. I also knew everyone who attended Rossan School, as did my sister Maria. Looking back, many from Aughavas would have had similar experiences, as kids from Aughavas attended a number of different seccondary schools. 1979/80 was a confusing time for me, as I remember in the early 1970s I liked disco and soul music, but keeping up with the times I got more into rock music, which meant renouncing disco and soul. I guess little has changed as youngsters like to be admired, but are equally scared of being seen as "out of time". Overall the music I have listened to over the last forty years has been a big influence on what I am now, but who I was then was a more complicated story.

Not long after starting secondary school in Moyne, I learned break-times were not like those at primary school, which included difficulty fitting into football games. It was during this time I was learning more sex education from fellow teenagers than through any appropriate channels. As for identity I was certainly no punk and I would have felt out of place wearing a ska suit in rural Leitrim. My strange interests and preoccupations made me a target for piss taking conversations and on other occasions I would tell people made-up and somewhat embarrassing stories, which made me a school clown without my realizing.

Personally my biggest embarrassment was the prospect of failing at school and being in a lower maths and English class, which would be humiliating. Soon the most hurtful event was being thrown out of German for failing my Christmas exams. So hurtful I have felt that I still remain angry with that particular teacher for his intolerance of kids like me making mistakes. This was both a humiliation and deep anxiety for me, being constantly told I needed a language in order to progress with my leaving cert and for future jobs. I think this may have been the reason I chose to repeat first year, as I heard many talking about the "importance of getting off to a good start".

Many pupils did not need academic education because they had the strength to do manual work, which did not apply to me, but I also lacked the brains for a decent career. The future I saw as very bleak, as I felt Ireland was very much in morale decline. I was fascinated with the good old days and stories my mother and granny would tell me of many young men who became priests. I guess this played a role in my wanting to join the religious life and wanting to move to a religious boarding school. Round this time my interests in football were decreasing, but my interest in music was more on the increase.

I never went to any discos as a first year pupil, as discos were seen to be a bad influence by many parents. Despite that I loved my music and I was starting to develop a music record collection. This opportunity came when I got my first summer job at my uncle's shop. While the vinyl collection was mainly rock and heavy metal, there is one record I wish was in my vinyl singles collection. U2's "11 o'clock Tick Tock" was one of the greatest records ever released and over thirty years later U2 are still one of my favourite bands. Yet back then when both my brother VG and I tried to buy the U2 single in Longford, they had never heard of U2. Growing up in County Leitrim in the 1970s and 1980s taught me much about good music and that people in Ireland did not always need to follow British trends.

The early 1980s saw a number of secondary school

changes and returning to Moyne had similarities to boarding school, like not being able to enjoy myself, going to the cinema in my leisure time due to worries of being made to fight at school. Returning to Moyne had one consolation: at least I did not have to receive grief from pupils twenty-four hours a day seven days a week. At least I was having normal evenings living back home with my family, although travelling on the school bus was often rougher than the school itself, especially when I was accused of being an informer. I did become an embarrassment to my family and, looking back now, it was not easy for some of the teenage members of the family. I'm sure it was not easy for some of my neighbours, seeing how I was behaving, and I must have tested the patience of many pupils. I think one of the worst feedbacks I received was:

"Stop trying to chat to girls that hate you."

It was a very confusing time for me and I became a target of fun, especially when I got my flask broken, tape recorder damaged, PE gear stolen and was a target for fights, while being called "a fucking wanker" became a non event. This was something I would not admit to in the early 1980s and I would go on to say many adults even now cannot admit to being bullied as children. Many would say it could have been worse and it was part of growing up and at least these were the days before cyber bullying. Still I was coming to realize I was a target for fun, but at times I wish I'd been more stupid so as not to notice. As here is something a friend of mine recently put on Facebook:

*When you are dead, you don't know that you are dead. It is only difficult for the others. It is the same when you are stupid.*

(Author unknown)

I remember a certain High Functioning Autistic kid getting laughed at by almost everyone because of having different mannerisms and unique interests. Yet this kid was very intelligent on certain topics and despite mistreatment by others was never rude to others and always spoke to them with respect. I hope that kid turned out well and in later years, when I first learned of being possibly autistic, I also learned to forgive those smart country folk. For I realized they, like me, were kids growing up with their own struggles.

Many kids found starting fights, being disruptive or even bullying others a means to impress their peer group and feel significant. While other kids work hard to fit in and not be the odd one out, indeed many would go a few steps further to impress and end up being laughed at. Writing in the twenty-first century, I wonder, is it fair that many kids are distracted by the disruptive behaviour of certain kids in class? Indeed, thinking of my time in boarding school, I wonder if the Brothers in their Christian charity took certain kids no other school would accept. Yet many would say that's more of a behavioural management issue than a teaching issue. I myself was no angel as I smoked along with other guys in the school toilets as a means to impress. I realize now I was different then, so an easy target for laughs, and targeting the weak or vulnerable even happens in many workplaces. As for those who laughed and took the piss, it was not always in malice, and in recent years I have thought if only I could laugh more at myself my outlook would be healthier. Looking back now, there were many good people that attended Moyne school and many were good neighbours.

Back then I could not admit I was bullied, as that would make me a further laughing stock and I'm sure many still find it difficult years later to admit they were bullied. Writing in the second decade of the twenty-first century, I still hear how difficult it can be growing up as a teenager and trying to be part of the cool crowd. Ari Ne'eman, when writing in volume 30 of *Disability Studies* in 2010 states:

*"Often the environments which educates our children tend to tease and bully someone for having a different kind of mind, which is as wrong as oppressing someone having a different skin colour"*

(Ne'eman, cited in Loud Hands, 2012, p.63).

My self-esteem was at an all time low and no girl ever wanted to dance with me at school discos. One of the big questions I used to ask myself was "do I really look that ugly?". I think one of the most confusing things I found difficult was why girls fell for guys who could be disruptive and liked fighting. Perhaps many young girls felt safe being with guys who were able to fight.

Those teenage years were only a few years of the early 1980s. Some would say why look back? In the early 1980s Ann Lovett died giving birth to a baby at a grotto in County Longford and I'm sure she died in such fear. Also at the same time there was a guy murdered by a gang for being alleged gay and the gang got a suspended jail sentence. Back then the religious establishment saw giving birth to a child outside marriage more evil than murder and equally many gays lived in fear, and I should know, getting verbal abuse for being alleged gay. Even in the twenty-first century there are many religious and political bigots in both Britain and Ireland who will not apologize for past abuses. Which is why those days made me feel empathetic towards the many undocumented oppressed and I have often said:

"I do not have to be gay to support gay rights. I do not have to be black to support rights for black people. I do not have to be an animal to support animal rights and I do not have to be a woman to support rights for women."

By 1983 I made a decision to change myself as I did not want to commit suicide or run away and change my identity. Yet from my Life Coach training I have learnt we spend most of our time not being ourselves. In order to survive, I learnt to be practically someone else and a few years later I often ended up with women I only would have dreamt of in my secondary school days. Over the years my disguise was influenced by family, friends and good role models who surrounded me. I think it's sad how society and peer pressure force many people to be someone else, which helps explain anxiety among many people forced almost to live a lie. Having experienced bullying both in boarding and day school and being called the "School Bollox", I felt I had no other option. In later years many of my vulnerabilities and insecurities would still come to the surface, but that was not a concern when moving to Mohill.

Mohill was my final school move and one of the greatest decisions I ever made, but perhaps I was starting to grow up and not have the early teenage anxieties. Despite this I lied about my age, saying I was younger, as I was fed up with being mocked in previous schools for being so stupid for my age. I also did not engage in conversations about previous schools. Perhaps it was down to being autistic and having difficulty becoming a teenager, as I learned in later years. One of the other reasons I moved to Mohill was a fear of not being allowed to do my Leaving Certificate if I failed my Intermediate when attending Moyne. Passing my Intermediate surprised some, especially getting my only honour in my favourite subject, History. History was perhaps my strongest subject when attending Moyne and that was thanks to a good history teacher. I learned something useful in history that not many kids were told in school, which was that Daniel O'Connell's battle for Catholic Emancipation meant little to the majority of starving Irish, who were struggling for a bite to eat.

Sadly history was a subject I struggled with in Mohill, which I think was due to lack of opportunity to study modern history. I had hopes of going to university to study for a degree in history, but I struggled in other subjects. I felt many schools did not like pupils learning modern history, as it concerned many ongoing political issues. Perhaps much modern history of the twentieth century and issues like the Mother and Child Scheme with Dr Noel Browne in the 1950s were not seen as compatible learning in a convent school. Sadly, other areas of hidden Irish history would make the news in future years.

*"History is often the uncensored, undisclosed news where often the truth and horrible bits were left out originally."*

(Myself, 2014).

Mohill played a major role in my social and moral development and social learning process. Those attending school in Mohill seemed to be more music cultured and pupils followed U2, The Smiths, Talking Heads, Simple Minds and The Pogues. In Moyne the pupils seemed to follow Status Quo, Meatloaf, C60 and AC/DC. Soon I was introduced to two influential books, *Wuthering Heights* and *Peig*, as a pupil. Perhaps one of the greatest learning experiences in Mohill was when one of the wonderful nuns, who has since passed away, said in class:

"When parents punish their kids, they should make their kids aware they still love them."

This explanation helped me, being autistic, in my relationship with my parents, but it did not always stop me from feeling that "certain people hated me". Many years later I would meet people who would believe "the world was against them", or have a fixed view of events a lifetime ago. Many of these people would become difficult management problems in the mental health service, but perhaps having a loving family and learning about love in Mohill prevented me from having a more dysfunctional outlook.

Attending school in Mohill made my transition to nightclub weekend work easier, as the nightclub was in Mohill and this gave me an opportunity to improve my clothing self image without sponging off my parents. It also meant I would not be mocked for wearing "out of date clothes". I did have disagreements with my parents, who felt I was spending too much money on clothes while not putting enough money in the collection box when going to church on Sunday. Growing up in Ireland in the 1980s was different from the 1950s, which often caused conflicts with parents. Yet the 1980s also had similarities to the 1950s, such as families being unable to afford to keep their kids at school and emigration. I must say now, it was much thanks to my father for getting me the weekend part-time job, but I was never that grateful then.

Much of my time was spent in Mohill. It was here I made many good friends, some of whom I remain in contact with to this day. These were great years growing up in Ireland and despite struggling to pass my leaving cert it did give me the confidence to move on into further education in later years. In addition I received further financial education lessons from friends which included learning what to drink in order to get drunk cheaply.

Other learning experiences included appreciating growing up in a big family and having younger brothers and sisters enabled me to keep up to date with the thinking pattern of younger kids. It is often said that "kids can get you hanged". I'm sure it's a miracle my mother did not suffer heart failure given the number of embarrassing quotes from her seven kids. Especially the time one of the family members commented about a pregnant women in front of many neighbours:

"That big fat woman is in the doctor's a long time."

I'll never admit to being an angel while growing up in Ireland and was often part of many politically incorrect jokes, which included jokes about dead people and gays, even though very little of the joking was in malice. Needless to say attitudes towards women also needed much more maturity. I remember a bloke sarcastically commenting about a certain older woman in a short skirt, saying:

"I would not put my hand up her skirt if I was paid."

Like many autistic individuals I did not have an answer, but the ideal answer would have been, "I'm sure she would not let you put your hand up her skirt, even if you offered to pay her". Many young guys had much to learn in their attitudes to women and, looking back now, it was often no wonder many young women went for the older guys. This was the mid 1980s, which saw comedies like *Spitting Image*, *The Young Ones*, *In Sickness and in Health* and *Blackadder* and the tragedy of AIDS became a weapon for homophobic attacks on gays. However, the good times in growing up in Ireland came to an end when it was time to move to England to seek employment.

The mid 1980s was a time of limited employment

opportunities in Ireland. This was also when Ireland had one of the most educated work forces in Europe. Actually I would go as far as to say there was such competition for jobs that political favours were almost needed for jobs like brushing the streets. Yet it seems not much different living in Wolverhampton and looking for work in the second decade of the twenty-first century. As for a career, in the 1980s I was still unsure, although my career options were to be a journalist, electrician or a DJ, but that was a dream and one thing I was not cut out for was working on the buildings.

*"Working hard for something we don't care about is called stress. Working hard for something we love is called passion"*
(Simon Sinek).

Moving to England meant learning fast; many times I would have missed days from school or gone in for a half day, I would learn that would be a sacking offence at work. Between September 1986 and February 1987 I was sacked from a number of jobs for offences such as being too slow or not learning fast enough. This was something I could not include when writing letters to my friends. Writing letters home was something I did not enjoy as it reminded me of my boarding school days. I might have felt hard done by being thrown out of German for failing my Christmas exams when at Moyne School, but this was a common thing if your work was not up to scratch. I remember watching Pink Floyd's film *The Wall* where the kids throw the teacher into the fire; well, I'm sure many workers would have liked to do similar to their managers and bosses.

The workplace (A Sub Department of the School of Hard Knocks) offered many young people freedom with disposable income. I felt it was no escape from learning and this became my motto for becoming a third level student in later years. I was like the 80% of the population who hated their jobs and learned that work is what you do when you are not enjoying your career. Indeed over the years I would find I would discover how job satisfaction would be a big motivation for me and recently I wrote on a social networking site stating:

*"Job satisfaction has always been one of my greatest motivations, as well as doing something I enjoy. This is something I experienced in some jobs, while other jobs made me depressed, anxious and made me lose confidence in my ability. Other motivating factors include job security, supportive and friendly work colleagues, good manager, predictability and of course being paid enough to pay the bills."*
(Myself, 2014)

In the 1980s, finding a half decent job was at times difficult, especially when asked about the ethnic origin of my parents and grandparents. While improvements have been made since, almost thirty years later I get asked about my sexual orientation in application forms. At least there is the option "prefer not to say", but I often felt like saying:

"None of your fucking business."

Certain jobs in 1986 became a humiliation and embarrassment for me, considering I had a decent standard of second level education. It was also embarrassing for many Irish working in England to admit they were earning very low wages. Still, I was grateful to England for giving me a chance, despite feeling I was not an immigrant due to being English born.When I returned to England in 1986, the only news item I remember was a particular police commissioner suffering a heart attack. I remember a black gang leader expressing little sympathy, due to the police commissioner's poor treatment of black people, but what I most remember being said was:

"I hope the bastard dies".

Despite growing up in Ireland for many years I was aware of improving race relations in England and I felt racist jokes about black people were unacceptable. However, many years later the statement "I hope the bastard dies" was something I would understand, being autistic and dealing with many people who wronged me. I remember visualizing the head of one particular individual exploding into pieces. Yet I often found when my anger cooled down, I would feel personal shame for having such thoughts. Often my inner personal struggling world was different from the outer image of someone working in England for many years.

England gave me job opportunities, care work experience and an education in the late 1980s and early 1990s. I must thank my aunts and uncles in Luton for providing a home for me, and as well as feeding me they helped make Luton a second home for me. Ireland still had a high unemployment rate then, but as the comedian Tommy Tiernan said, "we had one of the highest unemployment rates, but we were the happiest nation in Europe". Indeed this happy atmosphere was always felt when I returned to Ireland for holidays and like many I often felt the temptation of remaining in Ireland despite limited job prospects. While Ireland has in 2014 seen a return of limited job prospects, the country still appeals to me and as I said to my mother recently, "if I only enjoyed countries with good job prospects, then I would have never set foot in Ireland when leaving in 1986".

Limited job prospects became noticeable in England in the early 1990s and that was one of the reasons I decided to return to full-time study in 1990. I remember saying to an old girlfriend, "I need more education, in order to obtain a job where I could afford to buy a house", as the 1980s and early 1990s saw house prices in the south of England rise to unaffordable rates.

In 1986, when I arrived in Luton, it took me a few weeks to find a job and in 1987 Oldbury Hospital (Name changed for reasons of confidentiality) provided me stability and a job I liked for a number of years. If working at Oldbury Hospital had not worked out, I could have returned to Luton. However, for many arriving from Ireland that option was not so simple, as for many it was their first job and first time in England. Oldbury Hospital was a place of care staff and nurses, but many who lived on the hospital grounds behaved more like school teenagers. I think care work became too much for some people, as I realized in my nursing career many years later. Still, it was an employment opportunity for many coming from Ireland or the north of England. I also felt many young girls coming over from Ireland were open to the exploitation of certain older men. Indeed it was not unusual to see married men at nurses' home parties behaving like single men. Oldbury Hospital was a place of many staff in groups and I did not fit in well, due to working in a day centre, which many did not consider nursing. Yet in later years how many healthcare settings would be ruled by many staff in groups, making it difficult for others to fit in. Still, Oldbury Hospital was not where my future was going to lie and I was determined to have a positive career change.

In the early 1990s I wanted a stable future career, I wanted something that could attract a future girlfriend. Even though I had hopes of achieving a higher career, I don't consider the way my career turned out over the years a total disappointment. Yet, like now, fear has played a big role in my life and I was never someone for making risky decisions, for this was a poem I wrote in the late 1980s.

### Fear

Too scared to fall in love, in case I get attached.
Too scared to ask her out, in case she might refuse.
Too scared to run away, in case I might regret.
Fear is the word. Fear makes it stop.

Fear and depression was something I kept to myself, in the summer of 1990. I was waking up in a lonely bed while wishing not to wake up at all. I think my reality was going into another world at the time and I felt the most hated man in Oldbury Hospital. This could not have been helped by my increased daily alcohol intake and smoking dope. It was not until the end of the summer when attending Reading Festival that I realized smoking dope was affecting my state of mind. I was also finding myself staring at breasts of curvy women and it occurred to me what was happening to me. I had been in a secret suicidal state for much of that summer. I made an important decision. I decided to give myself a six month trial to live and shortly after that I felt a great weight lift off my shoulders. It could not have come at a better time, as I was due to become a full-time student.

Late 1990 saw a boost in my confidence when I became a full-time student in Public Administration, for ongoing assessments through regular assignments was something that worked for me when attending Luton University. Studying at Luton University gave me new friends and hope for the future. When I studied in Ireland a few years later the importance was still on exams, as that's how kids obtained their Irish Leaving Certificate. From my schooling experience exams were just remembering and remembering, but prevented many individuals thinking outside the box. While exams still have their uses, they should not be everything like in my old school days. Exams did have their uses for those who did little work in the academic year and then did all the study at the end of the year. Those who did course work but only graded in exams were not rewarded for the responsibility they took throughout the year. In football terms I have always compared exams to the FA cup, but continuous assessment to the League Championship.

Later, in my teaching role, it was interesting to see how continuous assessment worked for some children, and the self-discipline some applied to research, as well as the hard work and focus put into their work. Writing with an autistic awareness I have known some autistic individuals contributing to society with the right support. I think the same could be true for many kids who have different learning abilities and I was grateful for my time at Luton University, as it fitted in with some of my learning abilities.

*"There is something wrong when a person is able to do some things very well, but is not considered smart if these things are not connected with school success."*
(Howard Gardiner)

By 1991, as studying was progressing, fear and anxiety were creeping in about war. I was enjoying university with hopes for the future and moving away from the shadow of Oldbury Hospital. 1991 was the year of the Gulf War and there was concern if the war lasted there would be conscription. If such an event happened I would have moved straight back to Ireland, job or no job. I saw no justice in war and I even had disagreements with members of Sinn Fein regarding bombings and innocent victims being killed, but as one comrade said, "innocent people die in all wars". For me that was an acceptance of war. I was not prepared to accept it and the Gulf War, like many other wars, was for oil and wealth resources.

Like many I felt it was The Falklands War that kept Mrs Thatcher in power and during the Gulf War restrictions on the media were noted and many were disappointed with *The Guardian* newspaper for reporting like much of the establishment media at the time. However, over the last hundred years both Britain and America have experienced many wars directly or indirectly, be it the funding of many world dictators, the Cold War, Vietnam, Ireland and its long oppression by Britain, Colonial wars, Islam or wars on the working class. Yet whatever war there is, there always seems to be money for wars while cuts in health, education and welfare seem to be accepted norms of all governments. Many right wing thinkers and politicians like to call Britain a welfare state, a term William Beveridge never approved of; others could see Britain and many of the super powers more like a warfare state.

When the Gulf War started, I wrote a poem about war. During the Gulf War the Socialist Workers Party was not allowed their newspapers at Luton University. At that time I was taking a break from political activity with college and also working. I was also a little burnt out from being involved in the anti Poll Tax and being a Union rep when working at Oldbury Hospital.

### War

War it is a killer's game, the losers only die.
The winners live to tell, what are they fighting for.
Whatever's right, whatever's wrong?
There's no human justice, in a fucking war.

The last half of 1991 proved a confidence turnaround, as a four week break in Ireland rescued me from burnout and a near nervous breakdown. Oldbury Hospital was giving me too many haunting memories and I never got over the trauma of a relationship breakdown the previous year. Round this time I got fed up living in England and felt a desire to return to Ireland. While I enjoyed where I worked, I was getting fed up with top management's desire for us to provide graphs and data of the progress of the service users attending. Looking back now I still feel annoyed with that unnecessary paper work, yet it sounds like something of the many crazy ideas of psychology. Perhaps reading what a friend of mine wrote on a social networking site defines psychology:

*"Psychology is just a naked version of para-psychology stripped of magic and the meaning of spirituality. It was invented as a survival response to the 'witch hunt' as a replacement form which now serves the wrong master – the one who denies the origin of it within the ancient spiritual practices of transcendental consciousness. All the principles of 'how it works' and 'why' have been misinterpreted in the favour of the logical explanations of human behaviour and rational dogma and 'treatments' replaced with sacred healing processes of initiations, meditations, healing and transformations…which are attainable with less efforts and with more effect of positive outcomes, when resolutions are needed, rather than 'psychological' explanations of one's behaviour."*
(Anonymous, 2014)

Having passed the first year I returned to my Luton lodgings in September 1991 a second year full-time student with no job distractions. On my return back to Luton I decided to get more involved in the Socialist Workers Party (SWP), as I had started attending meetings a few weeks before returning to Ireland. I guess the event that moved me was the military takeover in the Soviet Union and I was curious what the SWP had to say. To my surprise the SWP were as opposed to the system in the Soviet Union as some so-called democratic movements. They described the Stalinist system as very right wing, as it was very conservative, totalitarian and hostile to other political systems. While many politicians in the West called the Soviet dictatorship "Socialist", I recently had the last laugh when reading of the thinking of a Conservative mind and even one *Daily Mail* journalist classed the Stalinist system as Conservative. After-all Conservatives believe in implementing "law and order" through state legislation and Conservatives have a mistrust of outsiders.

I no longer cared what the right wing press said, as I had lost faith with how the mainstream media reported the London Trafalgar Square Poll Tax march in 1990. For me personally, I was moving on from my days at Oldbury Hospital, as I was glad to be part of the SWP, a party heavily criticized at Oldbury Hospital. I was also developing further confidence in myself, as the person I was ten years previously had now disappeared. There was a gradual political change and by the end of 1991, many universities in Britain were occupied by students.

Luton University did not attract many potential left wing students. Indeed Luton was an industrial town that grew after the Second World War and one of its biggest employers was Vauxhall, where many of my family and relatives worked; and Luton was partly built by Irish immigrants from the late 1940s to the late 1960s. Yet by the time I was a student at Luton University, Luton had a Tory MP and many Irish voted Tory, so in some ways it was anxious times being seen as a radical student.

Despite the anxieties and few left wing student groups,

many students wanted to occupy the college. I remember being unsuccessful in running to be elected to attend the National Union of Students (NUS) conference when a comrade altered my speech, but I have learnt that this type of altering affects my communication. Still, I was elected for the Occupational Committee, receiving an adequate number of votes and no votes of opposition. Perhaps the greatest laugh was that one of the NUS members who ran for the Occupational Committee was the only one who got votes of opposition. Soon a number of the Occupational Committee students were meeting with the College Director and to my surprise I even appeared on the local television news, but not speaking.

Speaking in public was something I became involved in, as other students needed to be informed of possible occupation, but I received support from many other students never involved in political activity before. I was amazed at the type of students that supported the sit in as lectures continued as usual. The occupation, or sit in as some called it, involved a number of students sleeping in the college overnight and over the weekends. These were tiring times and with assignments and college work to do, these extra tasks led to occasional anxiety. With enough students involved in the sit in, I took one night off to stay at my lodgings and get a decent night's sleep. That night the sit in was disrupted by a number of students opposed to the occupation and the sit in and the police had to be called. Around the same time I was getting threats and harassments from some of those students because of my role in the sit in.

The University sit in was perhaps my closest experience to revolution and even many lecturers praised us. To be honest I don't remember any hostility from the Director of the university, but I do remember the NUS being unsupportive on occasions. Still, the sit in was a success and most of our demands were met. Yet I can't remember how long the sit in lasted, but it made me think how amazing that the British striking miners in the 1980s held out for over a year. Looking back now it was one of the proudest achievements in my life and I wish I now had half that confidence.

I felt my confidence increase after a Christmas break in Ireland; I was noticing my grades were also increasing. Luton University was my best student experience, as it was a college I had admired as a five year old boy and my late Uncle Francie McIntyre had worked on the building of the university. As someone born in Luton I felt I was contributing to the great works many Irish had made to the town over the years. It was a time I became known for being me and was not in the shadow of others.

The student occupation did not scare me away from political activities even though students spoke of the hard work it was. A few months later Luton hit the news again when former Prime Minister Mr John Major visited. I remember being involved in the SWP paper sale and many hanging around as Mr Major's arrival was meant to be a secret. Secret or not even Sky News had the event as its headline, showing Mr Major arriving in Luton and crowds chanting "Major, Major, Major, Out, Out, Out", as well as "thirteen years of Tory rule is thirteen years of hell". I seemed to be coming a long way in radical politics, but it would be some time before I would speak at a SWP meeting as I was still asking the questions at many of them. That still is a part of me and I think asking questions will be part of me till the day I die, as asking questions is often an intrinsic part of being autistic. Back then no one would have thought "I am autistic". Back then the hopes of Labour returning to government in 1992 were soon dashed with another Tory election victory.

I think the Tory election victory dented my pride a little and while the grades flowed, which led to a Higher National Diploma (HND) in Public Administration.. By 1992 my many relatives in England could no longer gloss over the real facts about the progress in England and many said it was the worst they had seen since leaving Ireland in the 1950s and 1960s. Trying to find work around Luton became futile and the hospital where I previously worked stopped recruiting staff. The last few weeks in Luton became depressing, with little work and no money.

My mood became so low I could no longer cope with being involved in the SWP. Many would see unemployment as having all the time in the world, for me unemployment has always been a time when my pride has been dented. Unemployment is a time of uncertainty, of not only "when I am going to get a job?" but also of feeling shame and unable to turn up to family and extended family events due to having little money. Unemployment is when your voice is lost and while you may have the time to study, you have not the motivation. I remember thinking this recession is manmade even though many would think it God made. I further thought that recessions are planned by certain capitalist elites to scare the working class into submission.

I was soon rescued from the paranoid world by the prospects of a job my sister found for me in Ireland. I'm not sure how grateful I was then, as I regretted leaving Luton, my home town, and I was becoming friendly with a certain female. While I had considered returning to Ireland, I wished to return more on my own terms. England was no place to live when unemployed and I was refused a grant to complete my degree.

Unlike Ireland, England was a miserable place to be

with limited job prospects. Like many I returned to Ireland and it was not straight away to the dole queue. Working and earning only £1.50 an hour gave me some security and the job was a useful learning experience. While £1.50 was low pay it was worth it to know that American tourists were arising at five in the morning to seek out the Leprechauns. Bundoran made me welcome and I am forever grateful to my sister for giving me a roof over my head. Working in Bundoran was a useful learning experience, as it was interesting that many of the hotels and catering establishments were centres of low pay, and many restaurants' staff consisted of child employees.

1992 was the year I returned to Ireland after gaining my Higher National Diploma in Public Administration, something that would serve me to further studies in later years. 1992 was also the year the biggest selling album in Ireland, "A Woman's Heart", was released. It was a collection of the best of Irish female talent and a fitting tribute to the women of Ireland. On a personal level I feel anyone who does not understand the significant role and contribution of the women in Ireland has never been to Ireland. In some ways 1992 could not have been a better year to return to Ireland.

A year later, in 1993, I achieved my childhood dream: being a university student at University College Cork (UCC) studying for a degree in Social Science. Cork was a wonderful city with places to socialize, but there was often no money to go out every night. My childhood dream would also expose some childhood nightmares, as written exams were once again an academic hazard. Despite spending only one year studying in Cork, it was a useful learning experience and would pave the way for my future career.

One unusual memory of being in Cork was that it was the first place where I noted pubs which stated "toilets are for customers' use only". I remember going to one pub where I had to request a key to use the toilet and to be honest it did not bother me, as I was only going for a quiet few drinks in the daytime. During the 1990s there were increasing improvements in disability access, but I felt it unfair for disabled people to have to ask for keys to disabled toilets especially. To me it felt like asking the barman permission to use the toilet, as well as half the public house knowing you are going to the toilet. Still, some would say prior to that many with physical disabilities would be placed on outings with people with learning disabilities. I guess a further awareness for me at the time was having worked in learning disabilities a few years before where many with physical disabilities needed incontinence pads or needed easy access to the toilet when travelling to town or going on day trips. This was something new to me then but over the years I have become accustomed to knowing of individuals with bladder weakness and the difficulties they often face. For often I question how far disability improvements have progressed in an age of beauty, perfection and progress.

While my time in Cork was twenty years ago, recently a store in England harassed my wife for going in to use their toilet. I was fucking angry with the store man as I felt we were treated like thieves, but I did say to my wife afterwards "I will not be buying any furniture in that store and I will expose them on public media". Needless to say I never did, just like I will not name the particular pub in Cork, as my time in Cork was a wonderful learning experience.

Studying psychology in Cork helped in my awareness

of mental health issues, but having worked previously in Oldbury Hospital meant I didn't feel I was being thrown in the deep end when starting in mental healthcare in January 1995. Prior to 1995 I was hoping for a change of career, but employment opportunities were limited in the early 1990s. I felt I'd done my time in care work, yet my care work experience was my ticket back to employment. So it was back to England on the boat, as a week's dole money could not pay a plane fare. Besides, having a return ticket for the boat meant if I got no work, I could collect the following week's dole money in Cork.

I adapted well into mental healthcare, but it soon became a burnout and the only area of interest was working in addictions. My interest in drug and alcohol addictions was my motivation for choosing mental health nursing in the late 1990s. Despite that, I often questioned how much of a say mental health nurses really had. For I would notice nurses would get the shit jobs, deal with the difficult mental health issues and get the blame for anything going wrong. Working in mental health was to teach me much about myself, like wanting revenge, holding onto long memories and intolerance of others. Thanks for the therapeutic interventions were usually given to psychiatrists, psychologists and occupational therapists. Working in decent mental health settings depended on what the agency offered and that often meant the stress of waiting by the phone for possible work and often the work came in the unsettled acute wards. However, that stress of work unpredictability was relieved by returning to Oldbury Hospital in July 1995.

My return to Oldbury was very much thanks to Devi an old friend and work colleague, as Human Resources tried to block my appointment. It was an opportunity to work at what I knew best; it also helped me confront the daemons of the summer of 1990, when I was stressed, paranoid and close to a nervous breakdown.

The daemons of the summer of 1990, as I realize now, were not just due to a break up with a girlfriend and then us falling out. It was the unknown consequences of being autistic, but also the result of teenage trauma and even being mistreated by certain individuals in early adulthood. To be honest I have found the falling out and not speaking to certain girlfriends more hurtful than the break ups. 1990 was when I became suspicious of many people and for myself I did not want to wake up many mornings. Even writing down my thoughts of persecution daily and composing poetry did not help at the time. It's difficult to know what was real and did everyone think the girl had seen sense leaving me? Especially as a so called friend of mine arranged a surprise leaving party for her. What was real that I was living in a tormented world and that was hell on earth. Now, I would dread to read what I wrote then, as all has long disappeared.

Looking back now, while it lasted a number of months, there was much anxiety and mistrust in the relationship. Yet this was the result of being made to feel I was inadequate to have a decent girlfriend. This was the result of years at school, especially boarding school where my self-worth was destroyed, and Oldbury Hospital did not help. This begged the question why did I return to Oldbury Hospital in 1995? Well, the answer was simple – in that black hole in the summer of 1990 the only thing that kept me going was working at the day centre and when I returned in 1995, I was returning to the team at the day centre, not Oldbury Hospital.

At this stage I saw the 1990s very differently from the

1980s. As someone famously said, the 1980s was the decade of big boobs. As a skinny boy growing up in rural Ireland in the 1980s, many of the desired women would be seen by some as rather large (now called voluptuous). Actually this came up in a conversation while chilling out after clubbing, when someone said "there are no Irish country women clubbing tonight". This was the mid 1990s, I was well into the house music clubbing scene and this was something I kept at a distance from my work life. I also kept my social life with certain friends distant from work, while when I met women it was not usually in the clubbing scene, as some would find it strange going out just to dance and enjoy music. I also felt Oldbury Hospital was no longer dominated by care staff and nurses living on the hospital grounds behaving more like school teenagers. Perhaps the mid 1990s had seen where even I had grown up in some ways too.

I was slow enough getting into the house music clubbing scene, but I had listened to much Ambient music in the early 1990s and when I got into the clubbing scene I became a Trance and Techno music fan. Some would have said had I stopped liking indie music? My answer was that I always had a varied choice in music, but still much of the music in the hit parade was shit. The house music clubbing scene had a friendly, loving atmosphere, unlike nightclubs in the 1980s, which had booze, hostile atmosphere and a competition to shift women. While the 1990s clubbing scene had not the atmosphere of the hostile boozy nightclubs, the drug use was a means to combine the dancing with the music and the good, loving atmosphere. As for hallucinating under drug use, I honestly don't have any experiences that I can recall. And as for what hallucinating is, New Insights, the Life Coaching School states:

*"Hallucinating often refers to our human tendency to tweak (in our minds) the information that we receive."*
(New Insights, 2011)

New Insights (2011) was referring to people's ability to absorb information and not drug use. The clubbing scene allowed many people, including myself, the freedom to express themselves and this could have even led to a spiritual experience, which did not please the establishment. It was also an environment in which I believe many women felt safer. For me, getting into the clubbing scene was better when I made my return to Oldbury, as in the early 1990s it may have destroyed my mental health.

Returning to Oldbury Hospital not only meant confronting some of my past demons, it gave me a greater chance to explore more of myself, as discussed later in "Journey of Faith". Working back at the hospital taught me to appreciate a regular Monday to Friday job and not having to travel to work, unlike agency work in London, where much travelling was required and only having very short notice of where I was going to be working. In many ways returning to work at the day centre the second time provided greater job satisfaction, especially when I could rework my Social Skills groups and make the teaching content more compatible for people with learning disabilities. Yet another issue in returning to Oldbury Hospital was that people with learning disabilities were more challenging due to many living in community care.

Living and working in the hospital brings unpleasant memories to certain people; for me, it taught me to switch off from work and over the weekends I knew where to go and socialize. Living in the hospital nurses' home and living in one room often made it easy to know where I had stored my books, music collection, personal paper work and clothes. It would be more difficult having control over my storage when I house shared in later years. While working at the hospital I studied "Changing Perspectives in Learning Disabilities" with the Open University, which looked at changing attitudes, but also expressed concern about how economic progress could alienate people with disabilities.

I learnt how economics can affect healthcare, as shortly before the general election of 1997 many people round Hertfordshire were becoming ill because the water company was turning off the filter equipment to save money. Although, I had seen many cutbacks in healthcare under a Tory government when working in care work in the 1980s and 1990s. Economics in healthcare and making cutbacks has often been the theme to running healthcare, often affecting people needing the care.

This was something I would become more familiar with in future years and I would soon learn how nurses would be used in that process. I often wished I could remain working in the day centre forever; I knew working with individuals with learning disability in the hospital would soon end. As more people were being resettled into the community, the days of the hospital were numbered.

In the late 1990s I started writing about my experience of moving to England in the 1980s. The piece was originally lost, but found again at time of writing. I found some pieces an eye opener, being unaware then that I was autistic. Looking back, I think the earlier writings may show a naivety in me, but even in the twenty-first century I still have much to learn.

# Moving
## (Originally written in 1999)

Moving to England was a move many from Ireland had done, but I didn't feel like those many Irish. As I for one was not born in Ireland, I was born in the Queen's country, England. Yet despite that, moving from Ireland in the 1980s, when nightclubs were as familiar in Ireland as in England, I still came back to England a much confused young man.

The year was 1986 and after more than fourteen years growing up in Ireland, I moved back to what I thought would be my new home, Luton. For I thought I had much right to claim it as my home as that's where I had been born and lived long before my many English-born cousins were ever born. During my last few months in Ireland I would have hoped to meet up with some of the kids I knew in St Margaret's primary school in Luton. Little did I know I would be different. Yet in my early months in England I realized my best years in Ireland were the last three years before I left. A pity the good times came too late, but a bigger pity was how Ireland once again ran away its many young.

Leaving Ireland was no big deal, as I did not see myself as an emigrant. Nor did I want to see myself like the emigrants of the 1950s, who resembled the band the Pogues.

But this was the 1980s and this was Thatcher's Britain. While I would never be one of Thatcher's adopted kids, I would still be paying taxes on less than minimum wages. Yet with no work in Ireland I was glad just to get work, whatever it was.

Luton was a town where work was scarce, but there was enough for me to get by. By the time I had been a few months in Luton I said to myself, "if only I could get women like jobs, then Luton would be a grand place". For the only time I could ever get women was when I went on holidays back to Ireland. Yet for the first few months in England I feared never returning to visit Ireland, as jobs were difficult to maintain.

I'll always remember my Irish landlady talking of never returning to Ireland and that quote was fresh in my mind on my first trip back to Ireland. To this very day I can say that my first return trip to Ireland was the happiest moment of my life. Yet while it did not bother me to return back to England, I began to realize that the only place I would be accepted was in the Irish pubs. But this was a strange experience for me, as pubs never featured high when I lived in Ireland. For social life in Ireland were night-clubs, trendy and indie music and dressing up. Yet when I went to nightclubs in Luton dressed as well as anyone, girls snubbed me due to my Irish accent. This was something I experienced also in workplaces, where Irish were expected to grin and bear racism because they were white.

Luton was a place where even second generation Irish treated Irish as much as strangers as anyone else. Racism against Irish was respectable when, after all, there were bombings in Ireland and we were seen as allies of the IRA. Yet I tried to convince many I was born in Luton, but that was all in vain. As much in vain, I tried to be part of the English establishment and I felt looked upon as an outsider. This often led me to ponder what would have become of me if I had grown up in England, as despite the English suspicion there were still the opportunities.

Opportunities were something I was grateful for then, especially when I left Ireland with a bare Leaving Cert and had only ever worked as a part-time glass collector in a nightclub. On more than one occasion I thought of returning to Ireland, but my first trip back there was one of my success stories. By the time of my first return visit I had been in an established job and due to start part-time college the following September. This was my high point as most of my friends back home had stayed due to third level education; now I was to have something in common with them.

As time moved on, trips to Ireland became more frequent, but trips for me were losing their thrill, as over the years friends from Leitrim started to move away and over the years it was time to start to let go. The isolation of being Irish was starting to fade when I got the job of my dreams, that of a care worker, with a move further south from Luton to Oldbury Hospital.

This was the late 1980s where with the rising Republic of Ireland football team and the continued rise of U2, everyone wanted to be Irish. For me it meant a lot as I always felt those born of Irish parents were as Irish as those Irish born. Yet some English were still bad losers who saw the Irish team as that of English born players and there were still those keen to point out how unfashionable the Irish were.

Fashionable or unfashionable I can't remember where I was put, but at least I didn't wear the Burtons (clothes shop) uniform. What I can remember was that I was in a job I enjoyed, had an improved standard of living and was now a part-time college student. The hospital also improved my self-esteem with English women, as some were finding me interesting. But as I planned to progress, the good times were not to last.

As I found my identity that of the leather jacket, ripped jeans and an awareness of the system, I saw myself more alien to many Irish, for I began to see the hospital Irish as a sneaky clique. By now many of my hospital friends only worked for a few months and then moved on. To add to that I was thinking of moving as my workplace was fast making a change for the worse.

While I was happy enough with what I earned, it was not enough for a mortgage; it was also lower than what I knew many people earned in Ireland. It was also a difficult job to convince people back home that England was not paved with gold. But while I realized far away fields were no longer green, I never thought I would become an English millionaire, as finding work was my chief aim first and foremost.

In 1989 I quit part-time college as pressures at work were making studying too difficult. For me this was a setback and my relationship with Oldbury was getting rockier. I was starting to feel out of place more and more. However, I discovered one good place and that was London. I used to go there during the weekends and had my hideout pubs round the West End. During the week I would also go to London to see some of my favourite bands. There I felt at home with my leather jacket and ripped jeans and now I was becoming more of a socialist.

By this stage there was a strong mood against the Poll Tax, and it was then that I considered becoming a member of the Socialist Workers Party. For at last I saw an English party that supported getting rid of troops from Northern Ireland. At this stage, while it was politically correct not to be racist or sexist, it did not stop struggles in the workplace.

I was not black nor was I a woman, but I was working class and saw many English economically worse off than me. It was also when I realized Mrs Thatcher did nothing for the working women of Britain. A year earlier I had started writing poetry mainly of my inner thoughts, now it was poetry attacking the system. However, it would be some time still before I would get actively involved.

One of the reasons for not becoming actively involved against the Poll Tax, apart from not paying it, was due to falling in love with someone. While that year I had been involved with different women, there was one woman who would not be forgotten too quickly. I met her at a time when things were getting better again at work and meeting her helped postpone my leaving the hospital.

While leaving the hospital was easy for many, it was not for me. To start I always said "I will never leave unless I have a better alternative". Besides, I had decided to apply for full-time college the following year and at this stage, economic stability was on the decline. I guess one of the things this girl and I had in common was that we were both career minded people and we both liked to go to London. Once again I felt things were starting to go well for me.

At the end of 1989 all was looking good for me. For the Guildford Four were released, Republic of Ireland had qualified for their first World Cup and I had now been living for a few months with a beautiful looking woman. I loved her so much that two weeks in Ireland at Christmas away from her was two weeks in Hell. But the positive end of the 1980s gave a positive outlook to the 1990s.

1990 rang in quietly for me as I left the Billy Bragg concert in London early in fear of not getting back to Oldbury. Still, I gave a donation to the striking ambulance workers before I left. With my girlfriend at her parents' for New Year's night I felt no motivation to join the folk round Oldbury. For I began to despise the Oldbury folk further, as many had decided I was no good for my girlfriend.

Early in 1990 I was accepted into Luton University to study for a HND in Public Administration. It saw the potential end to my days at Oldbury and my girlfriend was planning on moving away later in the year. For me it was a chance to progress in my career and not be seen as an "uneducated nursing assistant" for the rest of my life; besides, I wanted to explore more about life. However, while my career was moving potentially forward, I was becoming more insecure and anxious about the future of my relationship with my girlfriend.

The relationship ended after nine months and now every morning I wished to never wake up. I lost the girl I loved and it felt a part of me had gone. Oldbury Hospital became hell to be in, so to ease this hell I turned to alcohol and I became paranoid towards many who were my friends. Despite that, one place was a support to me and that was the day centre where I worked.

The day centre was to prove a further support as I was to have my job there when on leave from Luton University. University was to be a life saver, for staying in Oldbury full time would have given me a nervous breakdown. Starting University in October 1990 boosted my self-esteem and I no longer felt controlled by the hospital environment.

Moving out of the nurses' home in 1991 meant I had some secure accommodation in Luton when starting the second year of my HND course. It also meant I could take four weeks out to go to Ireland, after finishing working in Oldbury. A year of work, study and a difficult house mate was too much; besides, I had not gotten over the breakup of the relationship from a year before. However, the four week holiday back in Ireland was something the doctor could have ordered, as I was able to start second year with a fresher mind.

Second year at Luton University went better than the first year; in addition I became a member of the Socialist Workers Party and involved in a college sit in. Soon it was summer 1992 and obtaining a HND in Public Administration was no problem, but the problem now was unemployment. Two years before I wrote down my thoughts of being a dumped lover, now it was the thoughts of an unemployed ex-student.

Moving back to Ireland in 1992 was something I had not planned. To many this seemed a move backwards, especially earning £1.50 an hour, but this was 1992 and Luton was badly hit by the recession of the early 1990s. It was a move I never thanked my sister enough for, as she had a room for me in her house in Bundoran, where there was work. Moving to Bundoran proved more positive, as there was no moving back to England. It was while I was in Bundoran that I received news of no college grant and was unable to return to Luton University .

In July 1995 I returned to Oldbury Hospital, a move I saw as no step backwards despite views of others. For me, I had returned to a day centre, which was the reason I returned to Oldbury. On this occasion I returned as a care worker, but now I had a HND in Public Administration, a year at University College Cork and six months of working on mental health units in London. In many ways returning to Oldbury allowed me to move forward, as this was no longer the 1980s.

Like all good experiences the 1990s were not to last, and the days of Oldbury were soon to end. For me the decision was leave or be moved around, even though I wished to stay in Oldbury hospital for a few more years. Having now worked for many years in care work I decided to become a student nurse.

# Autistic Struggles
# Continued

History has spoken of many great people who struggled to bring peace to their nations and to the world. History has equally overlooked the many in the same struggle, be it journalists, who are continually imprisoned, tortured and murdered for exposing corruption and brutality, demonstrators attacked and killed, those victimized by mainstream propaganda, those victimized by unjust state laws and even certain faith groups branded as cults. The list could go on and over the years I have felt an anxiety for those many victims and a feeling of failure. I could do little for those who have struggled. For many this has included not having peace of mind. This was something I discovered most important for myself a few years prior to moving to Horsefield. Yet this was something I had not always realized. In the late 1990s, having worked for a number of years in learning disabilities, I felt I had worked with individuals who were getting more challenging and, besides, I had in earlier years worked with individuals who had a combination of mental health issues and mild learning disabilities. So moving into mental health seemed a natural transition for me, as I felt I had an understanding of being extremely stressed a few years previously and the difficulties I experienced growing up as a teenager.

Becoming a student nurse was the beginning of a new stage of my life. Oldbury Hospital restored much of my self-esteem. It was also while at Oldbury I restored contact with old friends from the early 1990s. I did experience a good social life in St Albans and London. Oldbury Hospital allowed me to make peace with the early 1990s, where I experienced many internal struggles.

Moving away from Oldbury in 1998 meant losing contact with friends, as well as family, in Luton. It also meant giving up work in the day centre, where I would never be happier in another job. While Stafford was a move north, it was a place I had a good feeling about and only one exam during the three years as a student nurse. Writing now, I feel if it were not for Stafford I would have never became a qualified mental health nurse. At the time of becoming a nurse, I felt "if you can't beat them, join them"; I also felt that after the revolution there would be a strong need for mental health nurses.

Starting off as a student nurse in Stafford was no easy task. After the excitement of moving to a new location, many realities set in. The first difficulty was to get over the break up of a relationship a few months prior to becoming a student nurse.

While Stafford is now a place close to my heart, at first I found the weekends boring due to a lacking clubbing scene like London's. For much of the first year I would make frequent trips to family and friends down in the south of England. In addition to that I found the first module as a student nurse quite difficult, as it was a change from the Social Science studies I had experienced over the years. Concentrating on anatomy and physiology was difficult and I felt, like many mental health student nurses, that the Common Foundation Programme was geared towards adult student nurses. Overall I noticed I was going through a depressive phase and I found it difficult to sleep many nights. I had originally planned that if I failed my studies, I would move back to my parents in Ireland and finish off my studies for an Open University degree. Still, this did not prevent the anxiety of failing my first assignment, as I was getting to like Stafford. However, this anxiety was soon no longer relevant as, to my relief, I passed.

Passing my first assignment meant I could possibly progress to further modules. Yet I also realized when visiting the south of England at the end of the year, I was not over a broken up relationship from a few months previous. I remember talking this over with one of my brothers in a pub, and following ordering an extra whisky, I stated my intention to see a counsellor. It was not an easy decision, but I could not have the memories of failed relationships causing me to fail my nursing. While I was hurt from previous relationship break ups, I did care enough for previous girlfriends that I did not want to discuss them in therapies. However, for privacy reasons, I wish not to discuss my relationships prior to meeting my wife, Helen.

Seeing a counsellor helped my self-esteem, but also made me see other, deeper, issues for the failure of relationships. This did not surprise me, as I tried to block out some of my unpleasant boarding school memories for many years. By 1999 I was able to share with the counsellor some traumas of the past, but it would still be a few years till I discovered that many of my relationship difficulties were due to my misunderstood autism.

Autism, I thought at the time, was something that accompanied learning disability and during my three years as a student nurse, I don't remember the word autism ever being mentioned. As a student nurse I had many placements on mental health wards, which were not always ideal due to negative memories of working on hospital wards, especially learning disabilities in the 1980s. Despite that, my experience of clinical placements was helped by working part time on mental health units as a bank nurse.

My outlook seemed to be more positive and I seemed to enjoy single life, with the attitude "all women are my girlfriends". I seemed to fit in well in Stafford, perhaps because it was a smaller town, unlike nearby Wolverhampton. However, as 1999 was progressing, with support from the university when I was completing and passing assignments, there was concern about my lack of communication as a student nurse on particular clinical placements. Despite that, I noticed that particular clinical placement unappealing even when I returned to work there as a bank nurse. In later years I would discover that my workplace performance depended on colleague relationships and job satisfaction. While I have difficulty recording when in 1999 all this was happening, I do remember my mood dropping and having to see a counsellor again. The greatest reassurance I received on my last session with the counsellor was "you're a good catch for someone". Those words were certainly true, and a few months later I met my future wife, Helen.

Meeting Helen, I often felt, was fate, as I was less than a year in Stafford, and it was because we were in the SWP at the time. As there was no branch in Stafford a comrade contacted me and made me aware of the branch in Wolverhampton. It was here I first got to know Helen. I think I may have been seeing another woman at the time, I can't remember to be honest. So as well as believing what the SWP stood for, meeting Helen is something that I have to be grateful to the SWP for. Over the years many right wing politicians and Christian Conservatives speak of the evils of socialism, but all I can say is "God loves us so much, that God allowed Helen and me to meet through the Socialist Workers Party".

Like in many branches of the SWP my time selling papers in towns on Saturday was interesting and Wolverhampton was no exception. I found the people friendly and many interested where in Ireland I came from, as many had ancestors who had come from Ireland during the famine of the nineteenth century. Indeed, even when Wolves played their football games at home there was never any opposition, as we got to know and drink with many Wolves football supporters. All this would be the start of a good relationship with Wolverhampton, as well as a good relationship with Helen.

Helen meeting me as a student nurse involved her witnessing my anxiety prior to the one exam and my three months on the forensic ward placement in 2000. Indeed Helen had her own anxieties, building a career as a Youth Worker with limited job opportunities. For myself, being placed on the forensic ward brought back memories of boarding school, as it had a hierarchy of service user bullying. The forensic ward placement ended in relief with Helen and I planning our first break together in Glencolmcille, County Donegal, Ireland. This holiday I feel cemented our relationship and less than a year later we announced our intention to marry.

In later years I would be criticized for my lack of empathy and being non responsive to individuals with mental health issues. Yet I remember one of the last assignments I completed was regarding the hospital admission of a distressed service user, who discharged herself the following day. My points of concern were that she was admitted at the end of the evening shift and then had to deal with staff from the night shift. The following morning none of the staff from the previous evening shift were on duty, so this meant she had more new staff to deal with. When I returned to duty in the late afternoon she was in the process of discharging herself. I felt the services had failed her, but I also learned the importance of nursing staff being on morning duty despite working the previous evening. In later years I experienced being a mental health service user and saw what I felt was an inequality of care delivered to some service users. Sadly I have also witnessed others having too much say and able to bully nursing staff, management and psychiatrists in getting what they want. However, back in 2000 I never saw myself as a potential mental health service user, as I was in the final months as a student nurse.

2001 started well as I got through my final assignments and passed whatever other requirements. I remember my final nursing assignment being on changing nursing observations. For while I agreed observations were needed in case of suicidal intent, I also felt certain that observations made individuals more paranoid and potentially more aggressive. I was to discover this a few years later as a nurse, observing someone who was an absconding risk and the individual then seriously assaulting me. Later, nursing in Horsefield, I understood how this might have felt, being put on Performance Management and the manager had staff watching me.

I remember the day I passed my final assignment, and it was only when I got home from university that it all sank in: I was now a mental health staff nurse. Being a staff nurse was one of the greatest joys of my life, thanks to the support of many wonderful staff on various clinical placements, and not forgetting the support from the university. It was this support I will always be grateful for. Thank you Stafford and God bless.

Celebrations were short lived, as finding a real job had to be faced, and I found applying for jobs more hectic than assignments. An example of this was failing a job interview when being the only applicant and it's quite ironic, writing today, failing a refresher complementary course. Although writing in later years I should have learnt that too many circumstances affect my work performance, even at the best of times being autistic means concentration is affected by too many distractions.

Over the years I have often realized I had to work extra hard at my studies, which can be stressful, plus there were other anxieties I experienced. This was possibly why I felt burnt out after three years as a student nurse. As well as burnout I had a bad feeling about the acute ward I was due to work on in Birmingham. Prior to starting work I desperately wanted to take a four week break in Ireland, but money was scarce and I needed the clinical experience.

I started work in Birmingham in October 2001 and it was a far cry from Stafford, as Birmingham was a city with the hassles and stresses of many big cities. I'm sure many were surprised how I passed my nursing placements and my anxiety got to such a level that when only two weeks into the job I was in hospital with a suspected heart attack. In addition I was due to get married the following July which meant there were many preparations and unnecessary hassles. While I adapted a routine process at work, I also learnt how difficult it could be readapting to the routine when off work for a two week holiday.

Over the next few months I seemed to be adapting to being a mental health staff nurse, but I noticed myself spending more time in the public houses of Birmingham and Wolverhampton on my days off. Getting to know the Irish pubs in Birmingham came in very useful, as it meant I had somewhere to go for St Patrick's Day in 2002.

Attending a St Patrick's Day parade in Birmingham was a heart warming event and is one of the biggest St Patrick's Day celebrations in the world, but does not get the recognition of London or New York. When I was there I thought of the grief and discrimination the many Irish had faced in the past with events like the Birmingham pub bombings. I also remember when I first arrived in England St Patrick's Day seemed a low profile event and it took some time before Helen realized the importance of St Patrick's Day.

It would be unfair to say working in Birmingham was all bad, for I had good mentor support, there were staff I could work well with and it was where I developed my confidence as a nurse. I was even coping with some of the challenges of the acute ward, which included working a terrible shift system and staff leaving regularly. But depending on the public transport could be anxiety provoking, especially train connections. Despite settling better in the work environment, after six months in Birmingham I started looking for other positions, which led to my experiencing job rejections, with depressing consequences. In addition I was missing Stafford and while I can recall now the impact leaving Horsefield had on me, I think leaving Stafford had just as negative an impact. Eventually, after looking for a few jobs I would accept a job in Dublin, almost at the expense of my marriage.

Getting married to Helen was perhaps my greatest living experience and I think Helen would say every year of marriage has seen our relationship grow. Marriage meant a lot to me as even in my single days, I was at heart a family man. Yet the weeks before and after our marriage, the acute mental health ward where I worked had individuals with greater mental health challenges, which became too much for me. Soon it would be even more difficult for Helen, seeing me off sick from work and then my moving to Dublin, leaving Helen behind in Wolverhampton.

To this day I regret that move, but I also felt that remaining working in Birmingham would have caused a difficult strain on our marriage and Ireland has always been our dream.

No longer did I feel a thrill travelling from Dublin to Leitrim, unlike when I was coming over from England on holidays. Now was the realization that Ireland was no longer a holiday escape. Work in Dublin became stressful and I was making as many errors as I had when starting in Birmingham. I experienced a further vote of no confidence when I was made aware of my communication difficulties. Management also informed me I was placed on an elderly mental health ward because research stated it was less stressful. Writing many years later, this is how my communication could often be described:

*"When communication works, it's a bit like following the flow of moving traffic when there are no accidents or hold ups. I guess my communication is more like rush hour traffic caught up in accidents and traffic jams."*

(Myself, 2014)

Some people may not see the funny side of my poor communication. Yet back then it was stressful as I felt I was working below my skills; still, it would later be a positive learning experience. Visiting Helen in Wolverhampton was something I really looked forward to, as I really missed her, being in Dublin.

Over the next few months I found myself struggling with nursing in Dublin and I received regular criticism from top management. I now felt that while nursing jobs were guaranteed, finding a job with satisfaction would be a miracle. This was not helped by a poor work attendance due to being off sick on frequent occasions. I was often off work due to frequent chest infections, which was probably not helped by stress. Stress and anxiety have often further enhanced my communication difficulties and I have often misinterpreted what has been said over the years. Yet, as I more recently learned, when stressed and anxious our peripheral vision narrows, our ability to pick up subtle cues fades and effective communication strategies get forgotten. Being highly stressed has often affected my rapport and interaction with other individuals.

*"Self-esteem is the most fragile attribute in human nature. It can be damaged by very minor incidents and it's reconstruction is often difficult to engineer".*
(Dr James Dobson).

The stress of being away from my loved ones seemed to draw no sympathy from top management. Especially when one of the top managers stated "what about the welfare of other nurses on the ward?". Little sympathy was expressed by management when I was off sick a few months later with depressive illness. Despite management personnel being mental health nurses, it was my first time on antidepressants and at one stage I thought I was going to be admitted to a psychiatric hospital. To be honest, over the years I have found mental health professionals provide quality service to the service users, but nurses with mental health issues get treated like shit. However, as I was to learn, there would be other places my communication would pose difficulties and often little sympathy was given for possible mental health problems. Yet all was not at an end and that was thanks to old friends Ann and Devi from my days at Oldbury Hospital, who were to come to my rescue.

My good friends were able to provide references, which enabled me to move to agency nursing, but I did not leave the hospital on good terms, when top management refused to accept my change in notice of resignation. Perhaps I was right when I smelt a rat and decided to hand in my notice a few weeks before I might have had to face being dismissed. At this stage some would say I have difficulty taking criticism and that management have a responsibility, especially in healthcare where public health is concerned. Writing now I have learnt to forgive those many managers, even though some would say I have not forgotten. Although I have often felt that management had little sympathy for my mental health issues that does not mean I am not responsible for my spiritual and mental wellbeing, which includes trying to question whether management actions were taken in malice.

Mental health issues became something of a concern for me not long after starting agency nursing, when I was assaulted by a service user on an acute mental health ward. I also learned that as well as agency nursing being risky and unpredictable, there's the stress of adapting to a new environment while being thrown straight into the deep end. I would go on to say agencies are often used for jobs no one wants and are an easy hiring and firing tool.

Soon I was back on antidepressants and Helen had to cope with my short fuses and door slamming, although it must also be stated that my autism was unknown then. Despite that, I was only on antidepressants for a short while and by early 2004 I was back in agency nursing, this time in learning disabilities and rather ironic that it was with the same organization I had worked for when I had arrived in Dublin. Working in learning disabilities made me feel at home in my area of care work and I remember this when I was on my learning disability placement as a student nurse. Work was enjoyable, but due to housing concerns we returned to Wolverhampton and thanks to my friend Ann a job in day care awaited me.

Working in day care in London was being back in what I worked in best, even though I would get hostile responses from some residential nurses, as to how I could work in day care and still call myself a nurse. This was their problem not mine and for the first in a long time I was in a job receiving positive feedback and my confidence was restored enough to continue my nursing registration. Despite that I don't think it was easy for Helen, as I was away in London for half the week after we had been apart the previous year.

Money was tight with travelling and accommodation expenses and earlier that year two people close to me died, one being my granny. Money became so tight that I felt we would be financially better off on unemployment benefits and during the week I often had no money to buy food. Having some roast chicken on Sunday allowed for a chicken sandwich on Monday and bringing down a few apples kept me going during the week. Weekends became something to enjoy, now working four days a week and Thursdays were like Friday, as it was Thursday evening I travelled back to Wolverhampton. Although occasional challenges occurred I gained valuable experience, including assessing people who would be suitable for the nursing home, but sadly the good times had to come to an end. To be honest I can never thank my friend Ann enough for the wonderful career opportunity.

The end had to come and perhaps for me the greatest guilt was leaving my friend Ann short staffed, as she had gone to such trouble to get me that job, but I'm sure she also understood family came first. Helen had showed me the job advert for a staff nurse near Wolverhampton; this was a career opportunity and more family time. This was also the chance to prove myself locally, as all of my career achievements seemed to have been in the south east of England. The job application was successful, but celebrations were only short lived when we received the news that Helen's only aunt had cancer, and a few months later she passed away. I was now finding the world a more confusing place to be, where rules seemed to be lacking and often people never knew what was right or wrong. This was 2004, a time my Catholic faith was becoming more important to me than my nursing career.

Over the years I have found the world a very confusing place to live in. Of someone growing up in Catholic Ireland, many would say "there was too much discipline and the Catholic Church had too much say". Yet in the twenty-first century I felt the opposite could be said and on occasions even more difficult to cope with, for this was Britain, with one of the highest teenage pregnancy rates in Europe as well as other concerns regarding crime and social deprivation. At this time I remember my views were changing with my increased involvement in the Catholic Church.

When it came to kids growing up, I believed in limited age of consent and I felt concerned about high sexual activity among teenagers. I did not see this particularly as a moral issue, but more as a physical and mental health issue. In particular I was concerned about the peer pressure and low self-esteem of many teenage girls. Many would say we teenage lads growing up in Ireland had more respect for girls, but I would say the girls had better self-esteem and if a bloke tried to push himself too far he would get a slap on the face.

My concerns for teenagers perhaps related to my own teenage difficulties with growing up. Living and working in the Wolverhampton area, I was also involved in the church youth group. Despite working with what I would call a well adjusted group of kids and knowing some of their parents, there was still vulnerability in many, and for the less fortunate kids there were few public services or state sponsored youth organizations. In later years I would become more aware of the impact on children whose parents were being treated in the mental health services. At the time I was back working in the NHS and I was coming to see the NHS as becoming too secular.

Although employed by the NHS my faith had become increasingly important to me and if I were to choose between the NHS and the Catholic Church, it would be the Catholic Church. As someone who only felt connected with the Catholic Church when in Ireland, it was surprising that Wolverhampton would play a role in that relationship and my journey of faith.

Wolverhampton for a number of years was more like a commuter town to me, despite the family home being there. Working near the Wolverhampton area allowed me to develop a social network in both the Catholic Church and the Wolverhampton Celtic Supporters club. A big part of my weekends was spent shopping in Wolverhampton market. The market in Wolverhampton had an eclectic range of stalls and seemed to accommodate the diverse community of Wolverhampton. This market also made me feel proud to be working class. Working Monday to Friday in the day centre made weekend planning easier.

Having worked in a day centre prior to my nurse training, I felt I could channel some of my skills from the 1990s. However, I had encountered difficulties I had not envisaged previously. For a start this was my first time working in acute mental health care community settings and some people being cared for had never been admitted to a mental health hospital ward. On a mental health hospital ward, there was little occupational therapy presence, but in community care they liked to run certain departments. Despite working in community care I was not a community mental health nurse. However, there were different professionals working under one roof and different professionals meant different opinions and different understandings. This created certain conflicts and stresses and one day sitting with my work colleagues I stated:

"Instead of a working together relationship as a multidisciplinary team, it's more like a divorced couple still living under one roof."

Unlike working on an acute mental health ward, where people were being treated for a certain length of time, in community care the treatment could be never ending. Some seemed reliant on the service, which seemed to become a concern in itself. My other concern was being a Care Coordinator for certain individuals, when I was not a Community Nurse. Being a Care Coordinator meant I was responsible for certain vulnerable individuals twenty-four hours a day, seven days a week. I saw it as like being a teacher having a class of twenty-five kids, teaching them and then being responsible for their home lives as well. Writing a few years later, being a Care Coordinator for certain individuals still makes little sense to me.

There were some individuals in my care I got to know well, some also cared for the welfare of certain staff like me. Around this time I questioned "do family and informal carers get much support?" There was also the challenge of dealing with more individuals with personality disorders and soon my communication became a concern, as well as not performing to grade E nursing standard.

On previous occasions there was a joke that if someone got a Grade E, it was E for eejit (a form of idiot)
and I'm sure that applied to me. Supervisions got so bad
and stressful that I had to contact my union representative and even the RCN, who can be sympathetic to management. On this occasion they were concerned about
the manager's behaviour. Despite being a mental wreck
and having grounds for making a complaint about my
manager, I did not avail myself of the opportunity and
was glad I did not, as I learnt my manager cared for me.
Despite my manager's expressing annoyance at receiving
good references which my performance did not live up
to, my manager never once suggested that I should work
somewhere else.

It was round this time I decided to see a counsellor as
my anxiety was escalating; I think this could have also
been a side effect of the antidepressants. I only saw the
counsellor on two occasions, mainly due to work commit-
ments; the counsellor did observe that I had a serious mistrust issue. More recently I discovered the impact could
have also been from fear and the following comes from an
article I wrote on fear:

*"Growing up in Ireland fear was something that practically ruled
me. Even now there are many people I still fear and I feel fear has
been enforced in this world"*
(Myself, 2014)

Fear was a big part of my anxiety, but my difficulty with
trusting has led to relationships I have been in breaking
down and affected some of my workplace relationships
as well as generally relating and interacting with people
throughout my life. Yet the issue of trust has become a
concern to many of the general public, due to increasing

news revelations of cover up allegations. Andrew Rawnsley writing recently in *The Guardian* newspaper states:

*"It seems we'd now rather trust an individual we don't know than a big institution that we have come to know much too well."*
(Rawnsley, A., 2014)

Actually my trust issues extend to me, as sometimes I don't trust myself to remember. As I only saw the counsellor twice, I never got to work on my trust issues.

While issues of lack of trust have played a major role in my life, it has not been all delusional. Often my anxiety increases waiting for buses to work or due to uncertainty of trains' or buses' reliability. I remember approaching work one particular morning and feeling increased anxiety, which was a frequent event. I also remember saying to myself "if I achieved Nirvana, I could walk through war zone situations and I could deal with whatever conflict". Writing now, if I achieved Nirvana, I would rather channel my skills into something more useful than walking through a war zone. Yet back then it had shown how much anxiety and lack of trust had taken over my life.

My then manager was someone who stated they liked a challenge and would have found me a challenge. For while I had experience in putting group activities together, both in learning disabilities and the elderly, I still had much to learn in facilitating psycho-educational groups in acute mental health. For the manager there was difficulty in trying to make changes and over the years I have witnessed where even unqualified staff can make or prevent changes in many care settings. I guess I felt this was stressful but starting in the day centre was not easy, as I missed my old job in London and I was experiencing increased anxiety as a side effect of the antidepressants. After a few months I started looking for other positions, but it was speaking to a work colleague that made me see sense.

Seeing sense it certainly was, as I remained working in that particular care setting for almost four years. Despite frequent anxieties when travelling to work, over the years I learnt to facilitate groups for self-esteem, assertiveness and anger awareness. As well as making certain changes I was able to see how much my life was affected by low self-esteem and anger. One of the good things about the job was having breathing space between morning and afternoon group sessions. Later when working in education I noticed the significance of teachers needing time between classes. In reality, time is needed to research if possible, prepare and organize, as well as time to be mentally and physically focused. Yet in other places I have had the experience of finishing a group or teaching session and then going straight into a meeting and this may be followed by an intense individual assessment or even admission. This was something I found extremely stressful and badly managed.

*"Growth for the sake of growth is the Ideology of the cancer cell".*
(Edward Abbey).

I may have already mentioned this, but I have seen many cutbacks both in health and in education. Despite that, managers and the public still expect higher standards, as well as experiencing greater hostility from service users. It perhaps explains why I have experienced burnout and meltdowns during much of my lifetime. Sadly, many community services, including mental health, are focusing the care more on individuals with more enhanced mental health issues. This often alienates those with minor mental health issues, who often need ongoing support. If the National Health Service is focusing on individuals with more enhanced health needs, then the service should be renamed the National Sick Service.

I must thank my manager for just allowing me to focus on groups and work at what I could do best. Indeed, my manager noticed some concerns and referred me to Occupational Health and eventually I was seen by a psychologist. The psychologist noted the effects of being bullied in my younger years. While not seeming aware of my occupation, the psychologist seemed surprised I was working as a mental health nurse. Dyslexia was something my wife, Helen, thought I might have and I still think I may have some traits, for recently I researched that dyslexic traits can accompany autism. At the time, the psychologist stated that going for certain tests would require being on a long waiting list. The psychologist further stated that I should not worry and I had done well, but the report did identify Dissociative Disorder.

Having possible Dissociative Disorder created anxiety about having personality disorder, and in much of my time in nursing the service users I got the most grief from were those with personality disorders. One of the great difficulties of working with people with personality disorders is that they are likely to get people who are trying to support them into trouble and are prone to making false allegations. In many care settings people with personality disorders have caused many divides and rules and disagreements amongst different professionals and multidisciplinary team members. Indeed, many professionals have ended up having to go on sick leave because of abuse and allegations made by people with personality disorders. In addition, some people with personality disorders who were able to manipulate certain managers got members of staff transferred from their workplaces.

That attitude sounds bitter and unprofessional but one

of my earliest encounters of someone with personality disorders was when house sharing. This particular individual was one of the reasons I needed to have a sick leave break back to Ireland and he caused many fall-outs in the house. This individual expressed anger at being wronged by certain people prior to moving into the house, but as it turned out he developed certain suspicions of me, especially when he desired a certain woman.

It was when working in community care especially that I became more familiar with individuals with personality disorders. For me, I learned it meant keeping a strong focus and an ability to think quickly. This has been difficult for me and problems with my communication make it difficult to work with individuals with personality disorders. Yet I also learned that many individuals with personality disorders often lead very miserable existences and I have often learned many have limited coping mechanisms, which leads to self harming, manipulative behaviour, impulsive behaviours, and erratic decisions and, on occasions, unrealistic expectations. While others find creating sympathy will mean people will feel sorry for them and in return they gain a feeling of love and connection from that sympathy. In recent times I have observed many more undiagnosed individuals with personality disorders, but for some it's a learnt coping mechanism and upbringing which can be looked at and can be changed.

For some the ability to divide and rule is often a means to surviving, gaining love and connection and feeling significant, where their lives are often tortured with mental health issues. Sadly, divide and rule is often used by governments, politicians, dictators, business people, psychologists and the media, yet few would consider that they have a personality disorder. I remember a business psychologist talking about how it was important to create divide and rule with products in order to create greater sales. Manipulative behaviour has led to many being victims of police undercover operations, being deceived by police lies in the name of so called national security. Yet for people having difficulty with personality disorders there are certain coping mechanisms and behaviours that they have seen as a means of survival.

Over the years I have often questioned whether some individuals have got personality disorders or Nasty People's Disorder, as I question how some individuals with personality disorders can manipulate healthcare management. Having a possible personality disorder was an anxiety for me, but I would have not let it change me. I would subsequently show that being autistic did not change me. Later I would be told that having a diagnosis of autistic would hinder my career chances and I felt the suggestion was really not to continue with further assessments. So it begs the question, what would have happened, having a diagnosis of personality disorder or schizophrenia?

Whatever the disorder I was not aware of being autistic at the time. I seemed to survive, but my wife, Helen, did witness a few meltdowns over the years. Despite that I feel it was my faith that got me through and every morning while I walked a certain route to the bus stop, I was saying my morning prayers. Over time I felt my future career was not in nursing, as I felt a desire to move towards the religious life. It was also round this time I remember saying to Helen much of my nursing career has been years of physical and verbal abuse, as well as unnecessary harassments from management. There were times I felt angry, thinking this is what I need to do to pay the bills and the mortgage. Having been in nursing and care work for most of the last twenty years, a change in career would not be easy. I found it difficult working for secular employers and this anger was felt in 2009, when I quit my Catechism of the Catholic Studies to concentrate on my nursing mentorship when nursing in Horsefield. The career I now desired was to be a lay chaplain or a Catholic deacon, and becoming a deacon would mean I would have received the seven sacraments of the Catholic Church. Yet in all this I realized my faith was turning full circle, where not many years before I was close to not believing in God and yet by 2008 I was thinking about writing "Journey of Faith".

## Reference

Rawnsley, A., 2014, http://www.theguardian.com/commentisfree/2014/jul/13/democracy-the-establishment-lack-of-trust-paedophile-ring-westminster?CMP=ema_1364

# Horsefield

Aughavas in Country Leitrim would always have been a part of me even if I had never set foot there as my parents were born and reared there, as well as many previous generations. Yet I also had the privilege of growing up there and there were many lovely neighbours, as well as a number of relatives. Aughavas became my place of worship, education and the Gaelic Football club was close to my heart.

Becoming a teenager meant moving further afield for my secondary education and after a number of educational changes, Mohill would become both my ideal education base and a second home. Mohill would also be where I had many friends, whom I am still in contact with to this day. I am forever grateful to Marian College and the boost it gave to my confidence. Mohill was where I worked over the weekends and this helped in my social development and enabled me to update my music and clothing collection, as much of my social life centred round Mohill. Sadly, the good times round Mohill did not last as, like many other young people, I had to move further afield and that was to England.

Writing now, I have lived in England for more than twenty years of my life, which has been divided between

Luton, St Albans, Stafford, Wolverhampton and brief stays in London. Despite England providing me with work, a career, a third level education and even a family, my heart has always been in Ireland. This is quite ironic as some people remember when as a child I always had a longing to live in England. Yet I have often wondered, has my longing for Ireland been because I found it difficult to settle in England or that England provided many disappointments in my life? For many years many of my planned holidays to Ireland gave me something to look forward to. However, Seth Godin has something to say about my difficulty in settling in England:

*"Instead of wondering when your next vacation is, maybe you should set up a life you don't need to escape from."*
(Seth Godin)

While living and working in Wolverhampton in the early years of our marriage, the content of our conversation when I came home from work was where will we move to? Sometimes it would be Ireland, while other times it would be Scotland or Wales. Yet a few years later we would find ourselves in the West Country which we would call home, and if I had a spare million pounds now it would be spent on a house in Horsefield. Horsefield is a unique, beautiful, small place with beautiful seas and beautiful countryside, but still not over built-up despite increasing new houses in recent years. It is also a place with nice friendly people and it broke our hearts to leave there in 2013 and the stress disabled me from working for a few months. According to my calculations Horsefield has been my longest set base since leaving Ireland in 1986. Which is why part of looking to the future is having somewhere I can call home for more than five years. However, many would ask how I ended up in Horsefield when my heart was set on Ireland, but to answer this I had best start with the year 2008.

In 2008 I was nursing in day care for people with mental health issues. It was a job with future prospects, but a future I knew not where. Despite doing a nursing mentorship course, my heart was with my other studies, the Catechism of the Catholic Church. However, although a career in the Church would be ideal, as a married man my only job prospects would be as an unpaid deacon. Many years working in nursing had made me question, was this a career for me. While I felt the NHS was safer under the Labour party, there was much pressure to reduce NHS spending. A Labour government, I knew, would not last forever and the Tories running the NHS would be like the Boston Celtic Basketball team expecting me to lead them to glory with my height five feet six inches. I had developed psycho-educational skills for working on self-esteem issues and anger awareness and control. These were skills I was grateful to have developed, but overall my relationship with nursing was not solid. If my relationship with Helen had been like nursing, I would not have married her and would have only stayed with her till something better came along.

A relationship with nursing is not only with people with mental health issues but also includes management and often difficult student nurses. While some may say, you were once a student nurse yourself, over the years I have perceived some student nurses as watchdogs who caused problems on different clinical placements. Still, some may blame the Schools of Nursing for creating such monsters and most student nurses I worked with were pleasant. Yet in 2008 it was once again because of a student nurse, and that other complaint "communication", that I was called to see my manager

Communication or lack of it has got me in more trouble than some career criminals visiting the nick (prison) and situations which would make me more anxious seem to clog my thinking process. For this was a time when work and course work had an impact on my Catechism course, which meant a lot to me. It was little surprise that something would give way. A few weeks after the complaint from a student nurse regarding my communication, I had severe chest pains and ended up at A&E in Wolverhampton. It was then I decided enough was enough and time to move on.

It was while I was two weeks off sick that I decided to look for future jobs. Looking for what I wanted was no simple task, but I decided to give myself six months and I was even prepared to drop my nursing grade to get what I wanted. As the two weeks moved on I began to feel better in myself, I even managed to organize a group I was due to facilitate at Wombourne library from home. Around that time I made one last online job search trip at the town library, prior to returning to work. One particular vacancy moved me – mental health staff nurse in a Department / Community home in Horsefield. In some ways it reminded me of one of the placements I was based on as a student nurse. This was where some people were treated on a residential basis and others on a day care basis. So this job in Horsefield appealed to me. Like on many occasions when applying for jobs I left an answering machine message expecting no reply. So low were my expectations that I had almost forgotten about the job when they rang me back. It also meant a discussion with Helen about the future.

Whatever the future, the return to work seemed less stressful. Perhaps deciding to leave took off some weight from my shoulders, I can't exactly remember. Over the weeks I seemed to be more confident in my job since starting there in 2004. Time was spent filling out my application form and moving to Horsefield seemed to appeal to Helen. Yet it meant departing from the church youth group, Helen's job, friends and the two cats. The two cats would be the hardest to leave, but we had learned that rented flats would not accept cats.

The trip to Horsefield was a day with nothing to lose; this was my first visit to the West Country, and what an opportunity it would turn out to be. Yet perhaps the greatest opportunity in the job interview consisted in mentioning my studies in Catechism, which led to being asked to facilitate a future Spirituality Group. Whether this led to my getting the job, I can never know. Spirituality would facilitate an important role well beyond my work life. Yet it still was a few months before life in Horsefield would begin, and in Wolverhampton there was much sorting out still to do.

Moving to Horsefield was not only a lonely experience being apart from my wife, but also an expensive one due to unforeseen expenses. Soon I was to learn that the easy going life chilling on the beaches did not apply to everyone, especially the many with mental health issues. Over the next few months I was to realize that instead of winding down after the Midlands, I was taking on an even greater workload. Soon my communication became a familiar problem and to my further disappointment my skills derived from psycho-educational groups in the Midlands were not valued in Horsefield. In addition I found the acute mental health ward seemed to care for depressed people, recovering drug addicts and forensic criminals under one roof.

Still, I was able to facilitate my Spirituality Group on a more psycho-educational group basis for a few months.

Indeed there were a number of mental health challenges Horsefield would offer, but it was a form of job promotion and potential career opportunity. I first thought where I worked was a therapeutic community but it seemed to create more of a hospital ward dependency in certain individuals. However, these negative reactions were not to last forever, as I learned Horsefield had its own unique issues, and over the next few months Helen would join me in the West Country.

Indeed, some would say Horsefield was a place I would learn much about myself and as early as 2009, when completing my mentorship module, I learned that studying for a nursing degree was not something to give you an ecstasy experience. Despite certain negativities Horsefield had much to offer, as Helen and I were living in an ideal location. Time away from each other was less permanent compared with when I first moved to Dublin, and living in Horsefield was a relief away from the urban stresses of Wolverhampton. It was not long until my interest in photography resurfaced; it seemed Horsefield was my inspiration for photography just like Sligo in Ireland was the inspiration for the poetry of W.B. Yeats. Which was quite ironic, as I grew up in the next county to Sligo, and Glencar in County Leitrim is included in one of my favourite poems by W.B. Yeats.

Working at the Department / Community home often created many anxieties, especially the decision from top management to have more student nurses. Like any working department with a number of staff there were often differences in opinions, but Mary the manager kept the peace, as she had quite a charismatic presence. Indeed Mary noticed I had communication difficulties, but unlike other managers, saying "communicate better or get out",

Mary referred me to Occupational Health. Despite that I found work at the Department / Community home could be hard, and after a year in Horsefield, having a holiday back in Ireland was such a relief. I enjoyed being back with my family in Ireland, but I said nothing regarding my referral to Occupational Health.

The results of Mary's referral led to my being seen by a speech and language therapist and then referred to a psychologist. I kept Mary up to date on the progress of my appointments, as she was a manager and was easy to talk to. I did notice Mary could be pressurized by top management, but also expected standards from all at the department. I remember early in 2010 discussing a situation involving a manager in the Midlands who had failed to deal with an out of control member of staff and while I can't remember Mary's response, I felt that would not happen in her home. That gut feeling was to have some relevance later in the year, as 2010 would be a year to remember.

2010 started like any other year, so much so that I can't remember the New Year coming in. Early that year two close friends of mine died and assessments for my communication difficulties were ongoing. To be honest I was unaware what I was being assessed for, but I had shared with Mary that my communication became more difficult when my anxiety increased. The reason would soon be revealed to me when I was told I possibly had Autistic Spectrum Disorder, but I would need to be formally assessed by a specialist. It was to become one of the greatest weights off my shoulder in over forty years of living. I was now feeling hopeful and felt I was able to learn more about myself. I now felt my communication difficulties were not all my fault, despite trying my hardest at work. Work colleagues seemed to have no problem when I told them I had Autistic Spectrum Disorder. However, the response from Mary seemed different as she said it was only a possibility. Perhaps Penni Winter writing in *"Loud Hands and Loud Voices"* in 2012 puts it well:

*"An Autistic child who grows up they know that something which is intrinsic to their very selves is so hated and loathed by those around them. They will likely grow to hate their Autism and themselves with it. Even if they don't have a formal diagnosis, it's still possible they will hate their weirdness or difference anyway and will likely feel almost as much pressure to be normal. They may come to refuse to identify as Autistic and deny themselves support. The chances are they will suffer from depression, anxiety disorders, deep anger and resentment, low self-esteem or other similar problems. Many will struggle to maintain their passing facade and will have chronic anxiety about being found out. They may have problems with drink and drugs, drop out of school or jobs, or even attempt suicide."*

(Winter, P., 2012, p.79)

Writing a few years later it's difficult to know if Mary's uncertainty of my autism was in malice, or perhaps it was with good intention not to focus on autism and use it as a hindrance. Mary grew up in a harsh working class environment in Scotland, almost as harsh as what my parents faced growing up in Ireland. However, at the time I took it personally and round this time Mary seemed unimpressed when I said "no" to a temporary move to another area. This created a deep anxiety in me as I felt if I were moved temporarily I would not be returning.

Soon I was to learn Occupational Health would not support me for an Autistic Spectrum Disorder assessment to London. I was informed this was not a work issue, which meant they were not obliged to support me. During the meeting I was informed that if I were found to have

Autistic Spectrum Disorder, this would affect my career opportunities. This made me question the future for autistic people in the work environment, as I questioned the impact it had had on my career to date.

It was around this time unpleasant memories were resurfacing and it would have been appropriate to have been seen by a psychiatrist. One professional I could no longer to speak to now was my manager Mary as I had began to see her as a typical manager and someone I could no longer trust. A recent quote I felt applied to many managers in the health services:

*"You become like the people you spend the most time with. Choose carefully."*

(School of Applied Spiritual Science)

As the year was progressing work was becoming a struggle to attend and I had what turned out to be a severe chest infection and this was making me feel drained. On one particular day I was hoping to finish work on time, but found myself dealing with a crisis with once again little support from the Community Duty team. Yet again another evening of not finishing till almost an hour late, as time was needed to write up what had happened. At the end of the day I was feeling totally exhausted; perhaps I should have phoned in sick.

The following day got off to a bad start due to the bus not arriving, which meant I had to walk to work. I was due to work a long day because of previously arranging to work on the acute ward when finishing my initial shift. Work was going well enough despite struggling with a chest infection, then Mary the manager wanted to see me for supervision. Supervision is something that gives me anxiety even at the best of times due to unexpected questions. Yet anxiety for me has been an ongoing concern and earlier that year I had that learned increased anxiety was relevant to having possible Autistic Spectrum Disorder.

During this supervision I was expecting to discuss ideas for a future Spirituality Group, but not on this occasion! I was told a number of concerns had been raised about my work ability and some would need to be highlighted if a reference were to be written. Mary further stated she had never had as many concerns raised about any member of staff. I stated, "it has not been easy having been assessed for possible Autistic Spectrum Disorder by the psychologist". Mary appeared to hear what I said, but then said the priority was to provide quality service to service users. Following this Mary stated I should work somewhere else and that there was a vacancy on one of the elderly wards. I told her I would like to work in the elderly day centre, but I did not feel reassured when Mary stated she would have to point out some of the concerns in a reference. She suggested I write and reflect on what was discussed, as well as contact the manager of the elderly day centre. I was unable to write about what was discussed, as I was too shocked by certain allegations. I could not believe what was said to me, as part of what was said was slander. Besides, time was limited as I had to go to work on the acute ward to finish off the evening shift.

A few days later I was seen by my doctor while off sick from work with the chest infection. I felt the stress from the supervision had led to the chest infection getting worse and there were good reasons for that, as I remember being in a black cloud of depression which felt more like a black hole. Actually I had visions of myself hanging from the hallway staircase of our flat and I had not felt as suicidal as this since I thought the same when I was living in Dublin a few years before. Back then I thought I would end up in hospital, but at least it did not last as long as in 1990, when the only way I overcame suicide was by giving myself a six month trial to live. But now I was a professional, and I had standards to live up to as a mental health nurse. But who could I turn to? I felt no hope and the only person I could really trust was my wife, but one of the visions of myself was the photo below. To be honest, even now I am not sure if writing this is right, as I wonder what it will do for my future job prospects. However, I also wonder, if any job drives someone into a black hole of depression for a long time, is the job really worth that?

I returned to work after one week off sick and not only had I a chest infection to cope with, but other events. For during my week off sick we received tragic news of our house in the Midlands getting completely flooded and that my uncle in Ireland was dying. When I returned to work I expressed concern to a colleague that I felt I was being pushed out, but I was reassured otherwise. Writing now, it could not have been easy for certain work colleagues caught up in differences between Mary and me. Still, I discovered Mary was prepared to listen to the service users and believe their allegations even when they were irrational. While it's vital that service users with mental health are listened to and cared for by management, I feel management have also a duty of care for their staff. During my many years in nursing and care work I have often said to work colleagues:

"How can I care for service users, if I can't care for my fellow staff?"

Over the next few months I carried on working but in a rather mistrusting atmosphere, and the house in the Midlands was in an unliveable state, which made it stressful staying in hotels in Wolverhampton during annual leave.

At this stage I wished to return to the Midlands as the house would be back in order at the end of the year, but job prospects in the Midlands were limited.

As 2011 progressed I felt moving to Horsefield had been an extra expense, pay decrease and extra work hassle. Extra work hassle included being on Performance Management over the last few months and I felt like I was being always watched so now I did not know who to trust. As I recently discovered, while Performance Management is championed by many businesses and managers, I have questioned its relevance in care work environments. It is also not without its critics and L. Freifield in http:// www.trainingmag.com/content/does-traditional-perfor- mance-management-work states:

*"Performance Management is currently a hot topic among business leaders and human resources, but it destroys trust between manage- ment and employee. Employees perceive Performance Management to be more punitive than productive and performance appraisals seek the negative in employee's".*

(Freifield, L., 2012, p.1).

While recently studying Life Coaching I completed an exercise on what someone needed to do to make me feel disrespected, which included:

- Deliberately pushing my weak buttons, due to Per- formance Management – for me the only place for pushing weak buttons is in sporting competitions like football or boxing, as opponents' vulnerabilities often need to be found to ensure victory. For myself, my work performance usually declines when I am being watched, threatened or put under fear. Usu- ally if I am in an environment where I am respected and appreciated I will then work extra hard. I don't think weak buttons should even be pushed in job interviews, even when many are applying for that particular job.

• Making me justify my disability to management on many occasions – this is almost like someone in a wheelchair having to justify why they can't climb stairs.

• Refusing to listen to my side of the story, especially regarding a certain allegation. Over the years in care work I have heard members of staff saying I am "on the side of the service users" and this often means listening to unfair allegations from service users. Yet allegations should be treated objectively, allowing both sides to have a say. As someone who has been a service user in the mental health service, it's nice to have supportive staff. However, staff in care work should try to be objective and supportive to all.

Galoozis (2011) in http://www.nfib.com/article/8-sure-fire-ways-to-demotivate-your-employees-55591/#. UxJ5N_QAX3M.facebook goes further when writing about eight ways to demotivate your employee. They include:

• Giving unachievable goals or deadlines. Once employees realize they won't be able to get something done, they'll think "I'm going to fail", as this was how I felt when having to mentor a student nurse. Mary was obsessed with what was part of my job description – mentoring student nurses. Yet throughout my years in nursing I have known of qualified staff who have never mentored a student nurse and would avoid students. However, I felt it difficult to say no and Mary also said it was difficult to make special circumstances for me.

- Implied threats. To be honest I felt threatened when asked to move to another area for a month, as new staff nurses were being brought in for six month placements. Then, in November 2010, when it was stated I should be working somewhere else, I was made to feel unwanted, paranoid and *wanting* to work somewhere else. This was further not helped by being told about concerns needing to be highlighted in the event of my manager writing a reference.

- Not honouring creative thinking and problem solving. When employees take initiative to improve something, there still should be some support. While I had ideas of what to do for the Spirituality Group, I lacked some of the ideas on how to go about promoting it successfully. Being autistic I did not have the imagination to ask relevant questions or advice when asking for support. When I gave a presentation on spirituality to the acute ward, the room was disorganized and I did not get enough time to properly set up, and as a result my presentation was a flop, which was immediately reported back to my manager. So I state the importance of support for someone with autism, especially where it involves a creative project.

Over those few months I had no luck receiving any support for having possible Autistic Spectrum Disorder. Despite those feelings of anger, anxiety and fear were present in my mind most days, while still not sure if I was autistic or not. Feedback was that support for possible Autistic Spectrum Disorder was only for children and teenagers.

Over the next few months I often ended up saying "yes" to tasks even though I was feeling tired, as I have never been good at saying "no", but felt aware I needed to please. Although the theory "mistakes are a proof you are trying", this did not seem to apply in the Department / Community home. This often led to slipups but there seemed to be no thanks for being flexible and despite increased anxiety I don't remember taking any days off sick. However, I remember reflecting on the many lucky breakthroughs I had had in my past career and secretly wishing for one at this stage, but it would not be too long till that would happen in an indirect way.

One morning in early August I was asked to have a meeting with Mary later in the day, regarding a student I was mentoring. Mary had included this on my Performance Management, despite awareness of my being possibly autistic. Still, I was unaware of the nature of the meeting. I was expected to carry out morning tasks, despite anxieties about having to see my manager. When I came to the office Mary read out an e-mail sent the previous day from the School of Nursing. The e-mail was regarding the fact a student nurse no longer wanted me as a mentor. According to the student I was not communicating well enough. The e-mail went on to state I "should not practise as a staff nurse". Writing now I sometimes wished I did sue for slander. Mary then stated she had lapsed with Performance Management recently, going on to say she thought I should be working somewhere else. Still I was expected to carry out afternoon duties and this was difficult especially when I heard service users talking about grief they had with employers due to mental health issues. At this stage I could certainly empathize with certain service users. At least, unlike in November, Mary stated she felt safe with me working with the service users and over the years I have developed many good therapeutic relationships with individuals with mental health issues.

That night I could not sleep, especially with the statement repeating in my head "should not practise as a staff nurse". The following day I was reassured by a colleague stating communication was the key to this job and I had committed no crime. This must have been difficult for my work colleague, who felt stuck in the middle! Yet I felt like someone up for a disciplinary and wished I had done something for real, like stealing; at least I would be suspended with pay and given time to make my case to a union representative.

A day later I met with Mary as planned and she asked how I was feeling, following her receiving the e-mail earlier in the week. The possibility of moving into learning disability was suggested, as I had earlier in the year hinted at this move, and this would later turn out to be the move of my career. When Mary asked how I felt about the move, I said "a little pushed out". I came home feeling more optimistic, but despite that my wife, Helen, woke up the next morning and did not know where I was, as I had gone for a long walk in the Horsefield countryside. To be honest, Helen went through hell seeing what I was going through and later I became concerned about the impact this would have on her physical health.

The next week Mary was quick to draw up plans for my redeployment and in later weeks she justified her reasons for my move as being due to increase in anxiety and chest pains. Despite Mary's justification I still think I should have been given a three month trial somewhere else, instead of redeployment. However, I also felt if I had not agreed to go, I would have been pushed out and that could have become nastier.

Recently I have learnt about the effects of trauma experienced by people with autism. For me this is relevant as traumatic events can easily recur in my mind. This was the case when I was often asked to see my manager, Mary, as over the years I have experienced many sackings and reprimands, both at work and in school. In care work and nursing this experience was less frequent, as I had never been asked to move before. Which is why I can't understand when watching *The Apprentice* contestants practically saying how honoured they felt to be what I call humiliated by Lord Sugar. While issues at work must be dealt with, I think there is much work needed in dealing with the sensitivities of autistic employees. This also includes moving people around. While it is said to be important to move certain people to somewhere more appropriate, this often benefits those making the decision while having a negative impact on the confidence and mental health of the person being moved.

My experience in mental health would come in useful in learning disabilities care as I often questioned the number of people with learning disabilities in mental healthcare and I feel there is a need for more learning disability nurses. Indeed, from my experience in mental health I noted many service users were never in employment and many never have completed their education. There has been much research regarding individuals with mental health problems that has shown increased difficulties performing everyday tasks when there is a deterioration in their mental states. This dates as far back as the 1990s and Karestan et al. (2009) writing in http://www.ncbi.nlm.nih.gov/pmc/articles/PMC2705657/ state:

*"Lower childhood IQ was associated with increased risk of developing schizophrenia spectrum disorder, adult depression, and adult*

*anxiety. Lower childhood IQ was also associated with greater co morbidity and with persistence of depression; the association with persistence of generalized anxiety disorder was nearly significant."*

(Karestan et al., 2009, pp.50–57)

It was a career turnaround in September 2011, with a move to working in a learning disability residential home. This was thanks to Marian, a wonderful manager who believed in finding what people could do best, and Marian had the qualities I felt necessary, which included:

- Listening to me without too much judgement.
- Encouraging me in what she thought I could do best.

In many ways Marian managed me in a way other managers had failed to do for many years. There were other wonderful members of staff like Jenny, Arlene and Kirsty, yet nearly all the staff supported me and made my last two years in Horsefield a wonderful experience. However, thanks could also be extended to Mary for arranging my move.

Working in a learning disability residential home allowed me to see the resettlement process in action, as I remember many learning disabilities individuals at Old-bury Hospital being in the resettlement process more than twenty years before. Indeed, I was to later see the impact on individuals' behaviour when additional individuals were moved in, as the home was almost becoming more like a hospital ward. Going back more than twenty years at Oldbury Hospital, I remember working on wards which had more than thirty individuals under one roof and writing now I am sure the large number of people and often distressing ward environments escalated behavioural difficulties in many individuals. So it was quite a relief to see an improved quality of life for many individuals, as well as quality of care in the residential home in Horsefield. Indeed certain individuals from the residential home were not only well known, but became part of the collection of characters of the community.

Working in the residential home made me feel there should be more, similar, residential homes for people with mental health problems, especially in other parts of England. Perhaps this is due to my years in mental health nursing where I got to know certain individuals who found community living difficult to cope with. Often I felt community care was not always adequate and many individuals who experienced frequent admissions to acute mental health wards could have been given more appropriate community residential care. Indeed, as far back as 1988 when the resettlement process in learning disabilities was still at an early stage and many Victorian asylums were still awaiting closure, I remember reading a national newspaper article exposing the difficulties of resettlement among the mentally ill.

"Mentally ill" may not be appropriate to say now, but it was a term used back in the 1980s and that was mild compared with other inappropriate words used in the English language. I'm also aware there have been different difficulties for Community mental healthcare compared with Community learning disabilities care. As someone who also experienced being a service user in mental healthcare, I can never be thankful enough for the care I received, especially in Horsefield. While being supported working in the residential home, I was also seen by a consultant psychiatrist who through much hard work got me seen by a specialist in autism.

In 2012 I was finally assessed by an autism specialist in London and after a two hour assessment the specialist was able to state that autistic tendencies were noted. Writing now, I think it was one of the happiest days of my life and one of the first people I contacted after the assessment was my manager Marian. At long last I did not feel like a suspected fraud and even the consultant psychiatrist seemed amazed, reading a seven page report, at some of the points written by the specialist. The interesting thing is that I had not long been working in the residential home when my manager Marian noticed autistic tendencies in me, and over the last year I have met a few other people who spotted autism in me. There was one person that truly supported me over those last two years and that was my wife, Helen, who was originally even prepared to pay privately for an assessment. While being recognized as having autism may not have been a career boost, it was certainly a boost to our marriage as Helen says she can now understand the "idiosyncrasies" in my behaviour.

Marriage became one of the stabilities in my life, as in 2012 Helen and I celebrated ten years of marriage. While work was busy I was just happy to have a good working relationship as well as a good relationship with my wife. Yet having good relationships is not easy for everyone, so I should be more grateful. I once said when working in England in my younger years "sometimes we have to sow our wild oats with jobs to find the job we want, just as people play the field before settling down". Some people may find this outlook inappropriate, but as someone who had frequent jobs over the years, I cannot condemn someone who has had frequent marriages, as like in jobs it takes a number of attempts to find the ideal relationship. I remember once thinking I would be someone in frequent relationships but never settling down. There was also a time when I felt "how can I have a stable relationship, when no job is permanent?" Writing now, I wonder how my family and community would have dealt with my being autistic thirty years ago.

2012 was also Olympic year and this also included the Para Olympics, but thirty years ago many people would have rudely called it the "Spastic Olympics". For the first time since 1976 Montreal Olympic Games I allocated time to watching the 2012 games, but allocated even more time to watching the Para Olympics. I also guess now being officially recognized as autistic I could associate myself with the struggles of some disabled people, even though I also struggled with certain mental health issues for many years. Yet it was amazing that now many of these disabled people were called "Super Humans" by politicians who were often responsible for the many cutbacks which affected disabled people. At times I also feared a new split between what would be classed the good and the bad disabled.

Reflecting now I sometimes think it was a blessing in disguise my parents did not know I was autistic thirty years ago, as there was enough stress having seven children growing up round a farm, along with financial pressures. At the time Helen and I celebrated our tenth wedding anniversary, we informed my mother of my autism. This did not surprise her, but I was glad we informed her as the following year my uncle died and my father was diagnosed with bowel cancer. On reflection I choose a good time to tell my mother about my autism, as it can be quite a complex syndrome to understand.

My parents' awareness of my autism was an indirect support for me and I may have also made them aware my IQ was only 90. Other support systems I soon had included the consultant psychiatrist and the psychologist to deal with past traumas. The psychologist helped me worked through some of my ordeals with my former manager, Mary, as perhaps Mary was a victim too. Whatever the effect I remember thinking if I ever saw Mary being harassed by men in the street, I would defend her from the attackers and I was even prepared to discuss with Mary some misunderstandings in one of the sessions.

There was further work on the darker side of my past that still needed to be looked at; in particular, the memories of a fall-out I'd had with someone over twenty years ago. This concerned the psychologist as I seemed to be speaking about the event as if it were yesterday. Yet with much work we were able to determine that certain failed relationships were the result of the trauma of boarding school many years before those relationships. Writing now many would say "forget the past", but an autistic brain is wired differently.

Part of having an autistic brain is not only having constant memories going round my head, but I can even have certain music playing in my head over and over again. To explain this: it is like comparing how a piece of wood and a sponge absorb water, where the sponge absorbs water quickly and squeezing the water out is also a quick and easy process. A piece of wood, on the other hand, absorbs water slower, but squeezing water out is a more difficult process and may require specialist drying. An autistic often experiences a similar situation, where it's more difficult to get rid of certain unwanted memories. I guess I used the wood example from seeing the contents of our house in Wolverhampton damaged by the flood; even now some of the doors still seem damaged.

Doors are often used in explaining life's progression, as in when one door closes another opens, and I think I have focused on the closed doors for much of my life. Working in the residential home gave me the opportunity to discontinue being a nurse and focus on just being a care worker;

after all I was not a qualified learning disability nurse. It was also thanks to certain people in Human Resources that Helen and I were allocated a new flat where I could work out my contract. Working in learning disabilities was a spiritual experience as I felt the individuals with learning disabilities had good souls. This all helped Helen and me enjoy Horsefield more, as we enjoyed the beaches, going for walks and socializing on occasional weekends.

To be honest the socializing scene in Horsefield was good, but it took me time to feel Irish and proud in Horsefield and during St Patrick's Day Helen and I preferred to go back to Wolverhampton. If Wolverhampton was not vibrant enough for St Patrick's Day then it was a quick train journey to Birmingham. Yet saying that, there were some decent Irish pubs in Horsefield where the Guinness was not bad. However, one great time to be Irish was the Six Nations Rugby and you needed to be in certain Irish pubs early, otherwise you would be turned away as the pub would be crowded. Yet the place Helen and I both enjoyed was the Horsefield Tavern, where we saw many great tribute bands to Madness, U2 and The Killers. The Horsefield Tavern was one of the few places which could provide good food, good music, good drinking and a good time.

The Horsefield Tavern was in closer proximity to us when we moved to our new flat at the end of 2012. By now we were living in a new flat and I was in a new position as a support worker, for this looked a good opportunity to stay till 2014. Plans for 2013 were to attend some complementary therapy courses, as well as being in a job with no transfer worries. By the end of 2012 I received a verbal apology from a member of staff from occupational health regarding a previous decision not to refer me for an assessment. Empathy was shown for the distress this had caused and having to wait for an assessment for almost two years.

Christmas was a wonderful experience working in the residential home, but it also gave Helen and me time to spend a few days together in a hotel to recover from the stress of moving to the new flat. Unaware it would be our last New Year in Horsefield, we did it in style by seeing in the New Year at Horsefield Tavern with the Red Hot Chili Peppers tribute band.

2013 started well with positive feedback from my first complementary therapy course in Thai Foot Massage and this gave me confidence to do further complementary therapy courses. However, this also meant being busy, as it involved frequent trips to London. As well as working extra hours I also remember attending extra courses in Horsefield and I needed to do some extra home tasks due to difficulties in my wife's physical health. It was round this time I made my three year work and study plan, but Helen stated this would only be possible if we stayed in Horsefield and this developed a terrible anxiety inside me. Soon I even noticed this affecting my performance on one of the complementary therapy courses I was attending and I was noticing myself starting to stammer in my speech again. Yet prior to that I should have smelt a rat, as despite living in staff accommodation I had to sign a contract stating I would continue my original five year contract as a residential support worker.

Over the years my anxieties have created unrealistic conclusions, but this anxiety was for real. Soon I was informed my contract would expire in October and this was largely due to my wife having too many sick days. Even though I had a satisfactory work attendance record. Over my many years in care work I encountered many employees who had frequent time off sick and even experienced uncertainty regarding employees' attendance, yet I don't seem to remember that going against them.

In some previous jobs I was often amazed how certain employees remained in their positions, which was perhaps why I felt it unfair being put on Performance Management two years before.

Sadly, at this time Helen was bedbound, sick for a few weeks, and I had the unthankful task of delivering her the news. I will never forget that day and I am still finding it difficult to forgive top management. I was informed of the news in the upstairs lounge at work; I wished I was a few floors higher so I would have been able to throw myself from the window. Even writing now I still think how cruel it was and how did they expect our marriage to survive such a strain after the stress we already had endured. I think the first thing that came to my mind was that top management never forgave me for my alleged poor performance as a mental health nurse. Many would say top management have to make tough decisions like getting rid of staff despite the personal circumstances. As well as having to finish a job I loved I also had to apply for work in the West Midlands and Wolverhampton area where jobs were limited so there would be many applicants for one job and there would be little sympathy for my poor autistic verbal communication. This is where I knew my communication vulnerabilities would be exposed, especially in job interviews. I felt it made no sense to apply for another job, as I felt the residential home was my job. To me it would be like my wife or partner dying and being expected to find someone new to fill their place.

Perhaps it's due to the consequences of living in a cruel world and perhaps I should be punished for the wrongs I have done, which have included not giving money to beggars on many occasions. Many staff seemed surprised and disappointed when I informed them, but others said it would mean having to extend the contract for other people working in the health-service. While this reassured me, it also made me angry that I was being set as an example. I remember feeling so distressed that I had to seek an urgent appointment with my consultant psychiatrist and now my past was haunting me more.

One of the results of having to leave Horsefield was a mental recurrence of the trauma at the mental health Department / Community home. I felt top management wanted me out because of my poor performance as a staff nurse in mental health.

I decided management needed to hear my side of the story and perhaps clear some misunderstandings. This was not intended to be a revenge attack, even though I felt I should be entitled to some form of compensation for the way I was treated. I was eventually informed that Mary had been shocked at what I said and I felt "not believed". As Mary stated, she shared with me some of her many struggles growing up in Scotland and had referred me to Occupational Health and this I can't deny. Looking back now, if Mary knew I had such struggles why did she agree to put me on Performance Management? While I was expecting no apology, I was not expecting this response. I just hope Mary did not hassle some of my ex work colleagues for being supportive to me. Still, there was one positive outcome: it gave me confidence to challenge managers' attitudes. As I had been made aware a few years before, there were lots more difficult managers I could have faced and my answer to that was, if there were other managers I would have taken the matter further.

As someone who has been taught to pray for those who wronged them I realize it cannot be an easy decision to move or dismiss an employee, even though I was not exactly dismissed. I guess this relates to a friend I know from my social networking sites who spoke of still being not happy about dismissing a particular employee a number of years back, an employee who had certain social and mental health issues. Even though this particular employee did not meet the performance criteria, he still feels more could have been done. It sounded like pressure from higher management and certain work colleagues. Personally I don't agree with Performance Management as it creates mistrust and low morale, and Human Resources managers who implement it are using the ideas of American business capitalists. Indeed, talking of higher management – there are many higher management who would like to get rid of employees who they feel are not performing well enough, and this includes employees who they feel are having too many sick days, and see their lower management as too soft on their employees. I have always felt that to obtain a position of higher management, one must be prepared to make certain ruthless decisions. One of my memories of moving over to England in 1986 was recent Employment Legislation making it easier for employers to dismiss employees. Sadly, for the particular dismissed employee discussed on the social network, further difficult social circumstances escalated. It made me think what would have happened if my mental health difficulties had escalated or I had even committed suicide when redeployed. Would management have admitted any responsibility?

Empathy is something important for all managers to have especially if there's an increasing number of struggling employees in the workforce. James Caan (2014) includes empathy when talking about "Top transferrable skills" every manager should have and states:

*"The soft skills of management should never be underestimated. If you want to get the very best from people you have to be able to understand exactly what it is that makes them tick. We are all complex and*

*complicated individuals and are motivated in many different ways. Some people need constant encouragement but others are more individualistic. The very best managers are the ones who are psychologically tuned in to all of their staff. Get that right and half the battle is already won."*

(James Caan, 2014)

I guess I am sounding more like a Human Resources manager, but I do believe in peace with managers, even though I am sure there are managers that live in fear and have regrets because of decisions they made. I have never been violent towards any person in my adult life and I despise the violent actions of men towards women. Violence concerns many who are autistic and violence towards police is not unusual, as many people who are autistic feel an anxiety towards authority figures like the police. For myself, I personally have little grief with the police, but many who are autistic are not in employment, and are represented well in the prison system. As a mental health nurse working on many acute wards, I experienced abuse from inpatients who often saw the nurses as nothing more than prison wardens. Although many were informal patients, it was often the choice of informal admission or admission by section. Over the years I have experienced depression and high anxiety, which has led to black and white thinking and even irrational thoughts that have led to difficulties in relationships and conflicts with management in workplaces. At least I felt no conflict with management working at the learning disabilities residential home and performance feedback seemed positive.

With the news of my contract coming to an end I found it a drag attending work and often questioned if I was well enough to attend work. Besides, why should I go off sick when I loved my job and why should the service users suffer, due to an unjust decision made by the bastards at the top? Some may complain at my disgusting use of language, but we seem to live in a world more offended by rude language than murder, starvation, being homeless and wars. Over the next few months I found it too difficult to put a Curriculum Vitae (CV) together; besides, work was getting more busy and staff shortages were getting more regular. Helen's ill health had an impact on her losing her job, but the stress she was under over the last three years impacted her physical health. Helen and I would have been busy enough without the stress of losing both our jobs and home, as even in the past when wanting to job change, job application completion could be very time consuming.

As time progressed we got used to the idea of eventually moving, but many would still say "you came to Horsefield on a five year contract". My answer to that could be "I'm not a state scrounger and besides I have much to offer". I could further answer that I had been unaware of being autistic when arriving in Horsefield. However, disability awareness allowed Helen and I to look to complementary therapy courses and, for myself, studying to be a Life Coach, as I had some experience through spirituality work and nursing in the Midlands. The last few weeks in Horsefield were busy with work and sorting out moving house, and in the process I damaged my left shoulder. By this stage I was beginning to look forward to returning to Wolverhampton and I would have found it confusing if top management had asked me to stay. Writing now, back in Wolverhampton, I have found many days too difficult to cope and I have often felt safer staying in bed. Often, the grief of 2013 has made it difficult for me to concentrate on my Life Coaching studies.

On returning to the Midlands I have seen so many

cutbacks in services that expecting service delivery is like expecting a football team to win when fielding only half a team. To be honest I think the public service cutbacks affect the working class most, while the rich get richer and pay little tax. Even church leaders have spoken out about their concerns regarding cutbacks, which affect many with disabilities and health problems. This concern is nothing new as Charles Darwin in the nineteenth century said:

*"If the misery of the poor be caused not by the laws of nature, but by our institutions, great is our sin."*

(Charles Darwin)

I say that as the religious orders were the original healthcare institutions and monks were seen as the first nurses. I guess that's what makes healthcare provision difficult in this present time; there is limited healthcare provided by religious services and even when I was in Ireland I remember religious healthcare providers having to change much of their care provision due to the dictatorship of the banks. Over the last year I have known a few people close to me experience mental health difficulties and as someone who has worked for many years in mental health, this gave me no wish to return to mental health nursing. Perhaps writing with feelings of anxiety and anger gives me a different outlook from when I am relaxed.

When I *am* relaxed not only do I feel positive but also forgiving of past events and my outlook towards certain people changes. It made me think that if misunderstandings and communication difficulties developed in our marriage, not only would our marriage have ended, but ended on a bitter note. Over the years I have felt anger towards managers, work colleagues and teachers, but conflicts were resolved or misunderstandings settled in such a way that I forgot the conflicts ever existed. As I write now, I see those recent conflicts which led to feelings of depression, anxiety and anger escalating, but now see those same conflicts in a different light and a more forgiving light. Yet also now, seeming rather unsatisfied about my return to the Midlands, it is perhaps a hard act to follow after five years in Horsefield. I certainly felt this more recently when I made a return visit to Horsefield, being greeted as if I was returning home to my previous workplaces.

Horsefield, like many places, allowed me to make some learning mistakes which I did not get punished for. Horsefield provided much beauty for my photographic collection, but the experience of taking those many photos was just as beautiful. My five fabulous years in Horsefield helped me learn many wonderful things about my identity, which included being autistic. Over the five years we were there Helen and I met many wonderful people in Horsefield including, over the last year, autistic adults, many of whom we hope to maintain future contact with. I feel Horsefield has a bright future for autism, even though many battles must be won. Horsefield gave me the opportunity to live in the England I experienced prior to the family moving back to Ireland in 1972, but combined with the beautiful countryside I experienced growing up in Ireland. In many ways Horsefield helped me grow as a person and the fact that working in Horsefield led to my autistic referral is something I will be forever grateful for. Wherever the future takes me is never known, but my five years in Horsefield will be forever remembered.

# Journey of Faith

Faith for many is seen as something connecting to the Divine, God, or a higher energy source. As someone I knew once said, "we are all religious in our own right", for this was 1990 when I had little faith. Sometimes that ability to connect to a higher source is not always easy as I remember Teal Swan once stating on YouTube "connecting with God is like tuning into a radio, as you must get the reception to perfect tuning in order to hear". Music can be a major connection point for me, as I have found myself listening to certain music at the highest volume, but then I may find other forms of music too loud even when barely at half volume. Sometimes connection with certain music has felt like a spiritual experience and spiritual health is as important as mental and physical health. While I believe in the importance of spirituality, I have also believed faith goes beyond the religious world. I guess a good example of this is when a sick person has faith in their doctor to get them better. I remember once an atheist stating that it was pilgrims' faith that explained the many miracles in Lourdes. While I had many disagreements with this person, we both grew up in the Catholic faith. Despite my disagreements with the Catholic faith over the years, it has been a big part of my identity and where my understanding of faith began.

I guess my journey of faith started like that of many, growing up with two Irish Catholic parents. Though that included the consequence of facing hell for doing wrong and that was very scary. Some would say that's being cruel to kids, but it was a means to learning and I don't feel negative consequences writing it now. Many of the prayers I learned I still say today and over the years I have learned the meaning behind those prayers. Going to church at an early age, as well as listening to the choir singing and priest preaching, was to influence me in later years. One of my particular memories was not being able to receive Holy Communion, and when I had First Holy Communion, I felt like the majority of people attending church. My first taste of communion was not pleasant, but I do fondly remember the preparations by Mrs Kavanagh, who helped me see Jesus as charismatic and a loving God. Despite that I often found Mass (church service) long and difficult to understand and often got into trouble for laughing in mass, but the routines did make it easy for me to follow in later years. To be honest church service and contemplative moments can often be too much for young kids, even many adults still finds church service too long.

As I moved towards my teens I became fascinated with the lives of the saints, and Jesus of course. Little was I to realize then that some of these saints would also be known as Ascended Masters in Spirituality. My teacher at Rossan School helped me in my thinking of my faith, which has still an influence on me to this day. However, I was often taught the faith by my parents and teachers in a very strict Catholic manner, which often gave me little time for curiosity about other faiths. Despite that I remember becoming quite fascinated with the Islamic faith. This was roughly in the mid to late 1970s and life was quite simple. Yes, it was true I struggled in primary school and wished to be in secondary school, but I think home life was positive, having my little brother Oliver around. I remember enjoying the weekends, especially Saturday, as it meant a morning sleep in, but Sunday was a drag, getting up for church in the mornings. I think the only major confusion for me was how I could continue to like rock music and football in the future, if I was to join the religious life.

My increase in general knowledge and world affairs had totally confused me and by 1979 my mother was pregnant again. I remember her saying, "the law of the church says the mother must give up her life for the unborn child". This gave me great anxiety, so much that I thought of killing myself if my mother died in childbirth. Yet this did not stop me going to church, for I think I shared most of my mother's views that "the Catholic Church has lost its discipline and is becoming too modern". I was now a teenage adolescent and some would say the age of innocence was ending, but shifting women, nightclubbing and taking drugs were still to enter my mind. However, my mind was more at peace when my mother survived her pregnancy and delivered a beautiful baby girl. If I doubted my faith before it certainly had been forgotten after the birth of my little sister, as I went to Mass daily when I was a first year in secondary school. Despite that I remember praying for the victims of El Salvador during a school Mass, as my vision of the Good America and Bad Russia was not as clear cut.

While I was beginning to question political systems and certain authorities, I was not able to realize how much of a clown I was making of myself as a first year student in secondary school. One of my questions on authority was how could the Catholic Church oppose socialism, which supported the poor and oppressed. Still my faith was intact and I wanted to go to boarding school with the intention of becoming a Patrician or Franciscan brother. The secular world did not appeal to me despite some liking for girls and a fascination for one particular girl, but in 1980 I was also enjoying the music of Madness, U2 and Joy Division while wanting to join the religious life.

Going to boarding school at Mount Saint Josephs, Tullow, County Carlow was my first step to the religious life. For many boys, getting up at seven in the morning and going to Mass before breakfast felt oppressive, but for me it was part of the faith. I guess I thought going to boarding school meant meeting like minded people who wanted to become "Brothers" and getting a good education for the future; little did I realize how different that would be. Boarding school for me meant having my personal space invaded, having items stolen, bed wrecked, salt put in my tea, school desk vandalized as well as physical, verbal and indirect sexual abuse. While I had been made aware of the strict brothers, I was not prepared for the behaviour of the pupils. Actually the brothers were good to me and I experienced no physical or sexual abuse from them. I think if the brothers had made any sexual advances on me I would be a total mental wreck today, as I was vulnerable then. In the early 1980s sexual abuse in religious establishments did not exist in many people's minds. However, thoughts of sex did exist among the boy pupils.

When starting boarding school I'm not sure if my sexual orientation was gay, straight or bisexual, but whatever it was I did not want to engage in any sexual activity. Having my private parts pulled at and guys trying to pull the towel off me after a shower was something I could not include in letters to my parents. Even if I had said anything it would have been ignored or I would have been accused of leading guys on. I guess some of these boys may have been victims of abuse or may have had difficult upbringings, God only knows. Eventually it led to my not having a shower during the last few weeks at boarding school and wearing the same clothes. I also remember fearing returning to boarding school after school holidays. So much that I did not want the two long bus journeys back to end, unlike now, when it is a relief to finish my long journey back home in England when travelling back from Ireland. Despite that, my greatest sanctuary was in being able to have private prayer in the boarding school chapel. As I now reflect on positive memories, praying in the boarding chapel was certainly one of them. Yet those memories of private prayer would not exist now if any of the brothers had made sexual advances on me.

In 1982 I returned to the local secondary school at Moyne, County Longford. Unbeknown to me then, the male-only environment at boarding school had affected my behaviour towards women, and by this stage I desired no longer the religious life but to have a girlfriend. . My inappropriate behaviour and the reputation I had developed made me the last guy any girl would be seen with, even at discos I very rarely got a dance. Looking back now I am sure many young people were under peer group pressure and there was no place for naivety or eccentricity. Now back at the old secondary school I no longer attended church daily and this did not please my mother. .

In 1983 I changed school again, this time going to Marian College, Mohill and to this day perhaps that's one of the greatest decisions I ever made. While I did not attend the morning convent Mass, I had no problem attending mass on Sunday morning and I did not believe in sex before marriage. My time at Mohill made me see value in education provided by the Church; I also got to know some wonderful people including my now old friend Michael Bermingham.

In 1986, having finished school aged twenty, I moved to Luton, England to find employment. I attended the church where I was christened and where my parents married. I continued attending church even after leaving Luton, but had stopped doing so by 1990. By now I was seeing nothing wrong with sex before marriage, as I saw it as two people showing love for one another.

It was round this time I became a Socialist and I saw the Church, government and business as one combined oppressive regime. This was when the Pope, Thatcher and Reagan were together going to bring down Communism in the Soviet Union, despite the fact many Socialists saw the Soviet Union as oppressive. I had come to see the role of the Catholic Church in Irish history written in blood, especially their opposition to the Mother and Child Bill in the 1950s and in the 1930s its blessing of the Blue Shirts to fight for General Franco in the Spanish Civil War. I saw religion contributing to the troubles in Northern Ireland and Islamic extremist rule in the East. Despite that I kept my anti religious views away from my parents. Furthermore, my brother Nigel was in the process of being ordained a Catholic priest and I did not want to engage in political disagreements when among family. Besides, I was finding the early 1990s a difficult time personally and falling out with people was the last thing I needed.

Some would say that during the 1990s I had reason to be negative as romance was either non-existent or disastrous relationships. Round that time my career was making little progress despite my trying hard with a few universities. In addition, part of the 1990s saw me unemployed and in dead-end jobs.

Over the years I have met many people who turned

away from God, many for different reasons. Many people get criticized for no longer attending church or turning away from their faith. Yet do the many who criticize those who have relinquished their faith ever ask "*why* they have done so?"

Despite the recession the 1990s were not all negative as in the middle of the decade I got into the clubbing culture (what used to be known as rave). I felt a great buzz taking Ecstasy while dancing to Trance, Techno and Hard House music. It was also a scene of lovely people and no one violently drunk, where I was well accepted and my self-esteem improved. Yet I also had a good time taking Legal Highs and one night I saw a sign which made me think there is more to life than this planet Earth. A question came to me: what if Jesus had said the following:

*"Laughter, song, dancing and play are a great part of the foundation for a strong connection to God. It has been a terrible development in religious practice, that self-flagellation, self-hatred and self-punishment are accepted as an appropriate means of elevating one's spirituality".*

(Anonymous)

While this experience did not change me, it had an impact on my spiritual outlook in future years. While I no longer condone illicit drug use, I often think there are many people trying to find meaning and have found traditional routes no longer relevant. It was also during the late 1990s that I remember watching the film Shadowlands, in which C.S. Lewis says, "I want to marry in the eyes of God". I said to myself, that's how I would like to marry even if I never returned to my faith.

By 1997 I was back at Oldbury Hospital working with adults with learning disabilities, and one of the many courses I started and never finished was my Open University degree. Yet it was the weekly residential school in Brighton that was to be a big learning experience. I learned that the Tories were a cross between Classic Liberalism and Conservative theory of thought. Unlike Classic Liberalism, Conservatism was not based on selfishness and one of its founders, Edmund Burke, was influenced by the Catholic Church. This would appeal to me in later years.

I discovered many of my old beliefs had not died and I would never say "Our Father" backwards. . I was informed that nursing in learning disabilities would decrease as pregnant mothers would be able to detect foetus abnormalities and therefore terminate. I felt cold inside, but then a few years before as a student at UCC, Cork, I had learned of Right Wing Sociologalists like Malcolm Murrey advocating abortion for women in dysfunctional environments. Whether these abortion attitudes influenced me in choosing mental health nursing in the future, I can't remember. What I do remember about 1997 is that I was enjoying life, being young, free and single, as well as coming to terms with certain sexual issues from my boarding school days. However, changes were forthcoming, as I wanted a change, having lived round St Albans for a number of years. That year I decided to become a student nurse in mental health and I think the influence was more due to the landslide Labour General Election victory of 1997, as there would be a future for the NHS.

By 2000 I was a student nurse and dating Helen, who was to be my future wife. . We met as members of the Socialist Workers Party (SWP) and Helen was into Spirituality. This gave me the confidence to admit to being a closet believer, even though I later learned Spirituality was not the same as a religion. I was also to learn that Spirituality was a means whereby individuals found peace, joy and love in their lives. In 2000 I was to have an indirect spiritual experience, which was to have a big impact in my future outlook.

That indirect spiritual experience happened when Helen and I were on our first holiday together and visiting Glencolmcille in County Donegal. As well as nice beaches and good pubs, Glencolmcille had me saying "have I died and gone to Heaven?". I felt a great serenity, as well as a connection with Mother Earth and the many souls who had frequented Glencolmcille over hundreds of years. I also remember being happy to sit with Helen at the Grotto of Our Lady. The short break bonded our relationship and I felt quite a different person leaving from when I arrived. To this day I still see Glencolmcille as a spiritual shrine.

Returning to England after visiting Glencolmcille I started to attend the United Reformist Church in Wolverhampton, a church Helen attended when growing up. It was there I first got to know Bill from Belfast, who would have an influence on my eventual return to church. As well as being church minister Bill would be someone I would regard as a friend to this day. I found the congregation friendly with a sense of community spirit.

It was that community spirit that made me want to be buried in Aughavas, even when I had little faith. Actually for many the church was where many neighbours met, despite many stereotypes of the drinking Irish and meeting in pubs. Despite that, attending church regularly proved difficult for me with working over weekends, as well as being dragged down finishing off work being a student nurse. I soon started reading more Islamic literature and came to understand some of the struggles Islam faced. While I never converted to Islam, reading the Koran helped in my understanding of God and even helped in some of my understandings of Jesus. My openness to other faith denominations meant Helen and I married in the United Reformist Church in 2002 in a mixed service with my brother Father Nigel involved.

Around this time I cannot remember if I attended Catholic Church in Wolverhampton, but Helen and I certainly attended the United Reformist Church. On occasions when Helen was working I sometimes attended the church on my own as being married to Helen makes me a part member of the United Reformist Church. One particular occasion I went to the local pub to watch a Celtic v Rangers game and the crowd supported Rangers. As a Celtic supporter I kept my head down, but I said to myself I bet I am the only one who attended the Protestant Free Church, which is meant to be the religion of Rangers. At this stage I was becoming more familiar with reading the Bible.

The Bible and the *Bible Application Handbook* were the only books I was able to take with me when moving back to Ireland in January 2003. As a socialist I wanted to know what the Bible said about the oppressed and I was drawn to reading Isaiah from the Old Testament and what he said on social justice. While I was no longer an active socialist I was still horrified at free market cutbacks, made by so called Christian governments, affecting the poor. As former American President Jimmy Carter said:

*"If you don't want your tax dollars to help the poor, then stop saying you want a country based on Christian values, because you don't."*
(Jimmy Carter)

Working at the hospital in Dublin meant better chaplaincy care for patients and working with nurses from the Philippines taught me how the Catholic faith is still strong among some young people. It was while I was living in Dublin that I bought one of the most influential books written:

*Enough Religion to Make us Hate* written by Victor Griffen.

It helped me see that religion had a role in bringing peace to Northern Ireland, as well as breaking down sectarianism. I felt Ireland should open its arms to all faiths, just as I would like to see people of different faiths proud of being Irish.

Later that year Helen came to join me in Dublin and to this day we still talk of the many places we visited. Shortly after Helen arrived we were treated to a day in Knock by my mother. The day in Knock helped me see people's devotion to the Blessed Virgin Mary and I felt her presence. I learned the significance of the rosary, that it was more of a prayer than a mantra. As a teenager I found saying the rosary as oppressive and pushing me away from my faith. More recently I have learned it is useful to spend three minutes a day in prayer with your children and no more. However, there was one decision I made on that day at Knock and that was to return to the Catholic Church. Although I attended church of other faiths, I remained undecided, but no other faith seemed to have a connection to the Blessed Virgin Mary like the Catholic Church. I found myself identifying with Thomas the Apostle, also known as Doubting Thomas, as I had been doubting and asking a lot of questions throughout my life. Perhaps that was the unknown autism in me. This renewed connection with the Catholic Church helped me become part of the Catholic Church in Wolverhampton on our return to England in 2004.

Working as a mental health nurse over the years was often stressful and challenging, but I think it was having a faith that kept me going. It was during the induction course with my new job within the Wolverhampton area in 2005 that I came across a reduced price book on "how to pray". This got me back into the prayer routine when I had not prayed for many years. Prior to that I only felt able to pray in churches, just as I have often found it difficult to do certain tasks if I found the environment unsuitable. The Catholic Church in Wolverhampton became important to me and for a number of years I was one of the Sunday evening youth leaders. It was round this time I wished the Catholic Church could allow priests to marry and I had hopes to train as a deacon. I guess if I was still single the priesthood could have been my other option, as I remember someone saying I "would make a better priest than a nurse". I did study the Catechism of the Catholic Church, which taught me not only about our relationship but also God. I think the most important thing I learned was:

"How can you love God, if you love Tom and Dick, but not Harry?"

The message of God being love influenced my future outlook. Perhaps one of my fond memories of working in Dublin was getting to know friends who worked in the St John of God Hospital, and written on their name badges was "God is Love".

It took me time to find out what is really love and after some searching I found one site, http://www.truthcontest. com/insights/love-sex-marriage/ , which included:

"Unconditional love is something dogs have, but humankind does not. If you give your complete attention, it will be more fulfilling for you and everyone, most of the time in this life and all of the time in the next. Spiritual beings are love."

Growing up in Ireland there was always a dog on the farm and I learned how faithful a dog can be. I would go on to state God's love is unconditional. I feel God is always waiting for us to return even when we move away. I feel love often needs much patience and personally I feel welcomed back by God, even though I should be more thankful. Love is what makes the world go round, it is what has kept many of us together and love has kept the world from self destruction. Yet sometimes we all still need to be reminded of the importance of love.

*"Love has nothing to do with what you are expecting to get – only with what you are expecting to give – which is everything."*
  (Katharine Hepburn, *Me: Stories of My Life*)

Love is something that has contributed to nursing and care work throughout history. Yet sadly when you hear of health cutbacks, staff stress and burnout, where is the time for love? Working in the NHS for a number of years made me feel disillusioned with too much secularization. One particular example of this was when the NHS sacked hospital chaplains. This view was not helped when in 2008 I felt close to a meltdown with work, studying my Catechism and trying to do the nursing mentorship course.

My disgust at extreme secularization in the NHS made me want to quit the service, and eventually I did, as my nursing career was to take a new direction – to Horsefield. At the time I was studying for a certificate in Catechism of the Catholic Church and this led to my being asked to run a Spirituality group when being interviewed for the job.

As both a career and a financial move, Horsefield was proving to be a move from the pot to the frying pan. As well as the costs of setting up our flat, there were also the costs of travelling to and from the Midlands. For myself, I felt pressure taking Helen from her old job and home, as well as from the loss of the cats. Work did not turn out as I expected as my previous group work on assertiveness, self-esteem and anger awareness and control was seen as no longer useful. However, one project I did get to work on was the Spirituality group, which is something I may use in my future work. However, due to certain changes, after a few months the Spirituality group came to an end.

One of the reasons the Spirituality group stopped meeting was that I began the FLAW course, which would enable me to become a nursing mentor. This course was uninteresting, time consuming and very stressful. Actually I would go on to say it was the opposite to bedtime erotic reading and that's being complimentary. Yet there was one positive from the FLAW course: when preparing my presentation for 'Integrating Students into Clinical Placements' I was sharing concerns about violence on clinical placements. Ferns (2006), in researching violent incidents against nursing staff, raises concerns that nurses who were physically or sexually assaulted in childhood were at greater risk of assaults by patients. I felt this explained why I had been assaulted and threatened on wards over the years. It was the reason I did not want to return to work on mental health wards and it led recently to increased anxiety and flashbacks. However, often the psychological welfare of nursing staff is unimportant, as staff must present as always positive, competent and respond to unpredictability. Writing now, it was perhaps faith's way of saying "you need to examine your career future", but I did not see it like that then.

Doing the FLAW course meant I had to quit the course for the Catechism of the Catholic Church and this made me very angry. Despite that, I continued to attend Catholic church on Sunday, but I was finding church more of a drag and a struggle. While I had my weekends off, often I felt too stressed and too tired to attend church on Sundays. .

I now needed to be more in touch with my own faith,

as I was regretting my job due to constant negative supervisions and regretted moving to Horsefield. In addition, having been referred to the speech and language therapist for my communication difficulties, I was then referred to a psychologist for further assessment. After a number of assessments, I was seen to have possible Autistic Spectrum Disorder, but this would need to be verified by a specialist in London. This gave me hope and I thought I would receive no more harassment regarding my communication difficulties, but the manager of my workplace did not seem very accepting of this and to add salt to the wounds I was refused a further assessment, which left me confused and in despair.

Returning to my faith taught me to forgive, but when feeling confused and in despair forgiveness is not so easy. I learned more recently that forgiveness for people with Autistic Spectrum Disorder is more difficult, as there are often many anger issues to deal with. Following feeling ill-treated at the Department, my feelings towards my manager were one of anger and resentment. As I write now I feel awful for thinking like that, but my thoughts were mixed up, and in particular, many bad memories were resurfacing from my childhood.

I later learned my IQ was only 90, which is often associated with violence in males, yet I have not been violent towards anyone in adulthood. Round this time I learned to forgive some youngsters who gave me a hard time when I was a child. As kids are still learning and as they are growing up they often target kids who are different. My manager was a professional adult who knew I might have possible Autistic Spectrum Disorder as well as mental health issues. Yet it would be judgemental of me not to forgive my manager and I am sure there is a link between forgiveness and Heaven.

I found forgiveness difficult because of the way I was being treated in Horsefield and in other areas of my past. Personally I don't believe in an "eye for an eye", as I see that as a form of revenge. Just like I make no apologies to say that all or most prisoners should have parole and there should be a theme of treatment and rehabilitation. When studying Reiki I remember hearing of a famous Hawaiian psychiatrist who worked in a forensic unit saying "I'm sorry, please forgive me, I love you, thank you". This showed a form of healing and allowed for those being treated to move on.

Perhaps one of the reasons forgiveness was not easy for me, as I discovered, was the anger inside me. Although it was implosive, it did affect much of my outlook, especially with certain people I often had disagreements with. One of my disagreements with authority figures and managers was that they always expected high standards, which I often failed to give, leading to angry thoughts coming into my head. It can be in a fit of anger or rage that people can assault others, leading to tragic consequences for all. I feel many angry people need prayer to enable forgiveness and find a way to channel their anger constructively.

Recently I wrote in a Spirituality Social Network article regarding abuse:

*"There has been much said about abuse and its effects. Actually I would also describe discrimination as a form of abuse. This is why I have felt that some discrimination I received in work environments was abuse. What makes it more difficult is how it affects people differently, which creates much misunderstanding and has made many people unable to speak about their abuse. As well as good mental and physical health, people also need good spiritual health. This raises the next question 'what is spirituality'. The answer to this questioned is something I found difficult to answer. However recently I learned part*

*of spirituality is 'What brings Peace, Joy and Love to an individual'. If certain abuses seems insignificant to certain people, then they need to realize if the victim has lost Peace, Joy and Love, they are a victim of abuse. Many years ago in boarding school boys would regularly try to pull the towel off me when coming out of the shower. While some would say it was only fun, but it scared me from having a shower for some time. Perhaps what made it worse were other more serious abuses I experienced at the time. It was something I could not tell anyone for some time, but in later years it brought up terrible memories along with other abuses. In more recent years I have learned what gives me Peace, Joy and Love, even though that has been invaded on occasions. I guess I have no right to judge others as 'only imagining abuse', as every one of us have different survival methods and a different spiritual path."*

(Myself, 2014)

I learned from the Jewish faith the importance of giving to charity. This includes giving to someone who may not be genuinely in need. The Jewish faith says "that's no longer your problem". Recently I thought how easy forgiveness can be if the other person says "sorry" or admits to being wrong. However, disappointment and anger can remain if the perpetrator is not sorry and denies any wrong doing. Recently I chose to be sorry to my wife, Helen, for exacerbating her ill health, but I could have blamed other circumstances which caused me to stress her. I buried my stubborn pride and I took the responsibility to say "sorry" to Helen, as it was not anyone else's responsibility. Just like I am responsible for forgiving those I feel wronged me; for if I don't, I think the horrors of the past will haunt me more. I know the feeling of wanting revenge , I do know what it's like to feel so angry that it affects my sleep at night. I'm sure like many I wish to be like those who forgive easily and I am sure Heaven is a place of forgiveness.

Heaven is a place, I believe, where everyone's talents

would be allowed to grow and where those talents could be used for the greater good. Heaven is a place, I believe, where those of whatever weakness or disability will be given support to contribute their talents for the greater good of all. Studying Life Coaching from New Insights, they talk about how people are driven to avoid pain and gain pleasure. Pleasure over pain – I found that as something useful to remember as I consider pleasure over pain has even played a role in many faiths, where Heaven, or some form of it, is seen as the reward for suffering on this Earth. While my experience in Horsefield could not be called one of suffering, it could have been the title of a book: *Journey out of Faith*.

A few years in Horsefield brought me much anxiety and loss of hope and I'm sure I was not giving good karma to the mental health work environment. As for myself I felt I was often struggling more than some of the mental health service users, but my spiritual health was at an all time low. . Over the next few months my anxiety and paranoia increased as I was then put on Performance Management. . After further complaints regarding communication I was moved and perhaps I should be thankful to my then manager for this.

. As faith had it, Helen had decided to contact some private autism specialists, but they needed a letter from our doctor. Our doctor a wonderful Christian and someone I call a walking saint, seemed concerned about my mental state and referred me to a consultant psychiatrist. It was the good work of the consultant that got me referred to an autism specialist in England, and by 2012 there was written evidence I was autistic.

Being autistic has given me a chance to know myself better and while it has not been a career boost, it has been a marriage boost. As for my career, I even stated to my manager when working in mental health "all I want is to know if I am autistic and if so, what job could accommodate me best". Many would say "God knows best", but sometimes when feeling down it's hard to keep that outlook. By 2012 I was in a job I loved, as I was now working in a learning disability residential home. The manager, Marian, was very supportive, but as I said to her on one occasion, "it will take a long time for me to trust another manager". It was interesting working in learning disabilities, unlike in the 1990s, as I now saw individuals with learning disabilities having a close relationship with God. Some would say that this positive outlook was due to working with good staff and having a good manager, but whatever the answer I thanked God for the lucky breakthrough.

. This was my first time working in learning disabilities residential care. Despite moving away from Monday to Friday set hours, shift hours did not bother me and even working sleep in shifts fitted round my church attendance some Sunday mornings.

As the year moved on I got more into complementary therapy and even got the feedback that I had healing hands. Despite that on some occasions I felt I had a useful non-verbal presence and was sometimes amazed when people would come and talk to me. I had become aware that lack of spirituality in the workplace environment could be due to lack of communication leading to misunderstandings and leading to bad karma in that environment. Over the years I have felt good spiritual care is part of people's care, but good karma in that environment is part of a safe environment and a carer having peace of mind and feeling spirituality fulfilled is part of that healing process.

My wife, Helen, has played a major role in my spiritual development and when we went on a meditation day I felt a spiritual experience similar to when I took herbal highs many years before, but I have experienced a closer bond with the Blessed Virgin Mary. Yet I also remember when I took certain drugs I developed a certain positive outlook and recently I have begun to think it was not just the drugs, but the ability to meditate and be in nice surroundings with nice music and nice people. Indeed meditation was not totally new to me, as I was aware of the importance of chill-out and relaxation music from my clubbing days, but I have also been involved in facilitating relaxation sessions in both mental health and learning disabilities care.

. Being autistic has allowed me to focus on certain tasks over the years. I see autism as nothing short of a gift from God. It is true autism is a disability and I remember when in university a young paralysed lady progressing well with her degree. I felt no pity for her because at least she had the mental capacity to learn, unlike myself. Autism is also classed as a "differability", but this world makes autism a disability. As the world has moved forward we have seen how many disabled people have progressed. .

A consequence of having autism was that it was not practical to continue in mental health nursing. Yet over the last year I have been looking towards complemen-tary therapies and their use as a holistic therapy for many physical, mental and emotional ailments. I have found that complementary therapies have helped in both my confidence and my spiritual growth. They have also allowed me to connect better with different faiths . Indeed my wife, Helen, has admired The Virgin Mary, or Mother Mary, and has joined me in saying the rosary on a number of occasions. Although we are a mixed marriage, I don't think I could have married anyone with so much respect for the Catholic faith.

Many may find the Catholic Church strange with all

its statues and various religious pictures. This is something that has never bothered me and while I have many disagreements with the Catholic Church, I do not apologize for the presence of statues. I feel it reminds us that as humans we are not perfect and sometimes we need objects and buildings to keep our focus. Complementary therapy teaches the importance of positive energy and overcoming negative energies. Over the years I have been in places, including workplaces, where I felt negative energies, but I remember coming home from church in Horsefield one Sunday and telling my wife, Helen, how I felt positive energy there.

Positive energies continue in churches, even in Wolverhampton, as going to church on Sundays is one of the positive consolations of returning to the Midlands. Wolverhampton is not an ideal location for an unemployed writer, as writers often live in inspirational locations. Still, Wolverhampton has not been a bad location for thought gathering and practising complementary therapies and this has given Helen and me a greater chance to work together. Hopi ear candling was one such example, which also meant having the right equipment to do future practice sessions. It was while shopping for this equipment that I decided to call in to a particular bookshop, The Works.

The Works has sold many interesting books that have piled up in my book collection and once again that collection would continue to grow. As well as getting some stationery for our printer, I decided to check the audio book section and on sale was *Stairways to Heaven* written by Lorna Byrne. This was the first time I had heard of Lorna Byrne and her books have been Angel Therapy for me since. So impressed was I that I listened to *Stairways to Heaven* twice in one day, for it was like a new revelation had come into my life. For over the years I feel many people have received important messages from above and this includes the messages to Kathryn E May and Rael. I feel God communicates the message to people in a way they understand best, so they can communicate that message.

One of the great things about Lorna Byrne is that she has spoken a lot about religious unity and that angels have no religion. Awareness of other religions and multi-faith unity has been important to me for many years and I don't think that is due to being in a mixed marriage. Over the years I have found it interesting to see how other faiths worship and how they relate to God. It's been a desire of mine to see a greater unity in faiths and many would feel the devil has an easy job with so much division and infighting on this Earth. Even looking back at what anxiety has done in my life looks more like the devil's ambition.

What anxiety wants for my life? Or what's anxiety ambition?

- To focus on the negative outcome.
- Not to enjoy myself.
- To be always distracted.
- To feel guilty.
- To not relax and end up not sleeping well.
- To not be "I'm okay, you're okay".
- To feel regularly angry and have thoughts of wanting to smash up certainplaces.
- To say "yes" when I should say "no" to certain requests.
- To have no confidence.
- Stereotype thinking and mistrust.
- To be avoidant.
- Not communicating effectively with others.

As my faith continues its journey, it has taken its twists and turns and sometimes not to everyone's satisfaction. Over

the last year I have come to see how the increasing awareness of angels is something that can bring many faiths
together. The presence of angels has played an important
role for many practising in complementary therapy and
I feel the angels have prevented me from making many
mistakes over the years. Having a faith and believing in
a higher being has been something difficult to mention,
but many practising in complementary therapy are very
open minded and accepting. Yet it is sad that the Catholic
Church has an opposition to Reiki and practising complementary therapy is something I avoid in family discus-
sions. Reiki is one of the great therapies I have found very
useful and a friend of mine on a social network gave an
ideal definition of Reiki.

*"Reiki is a simple, natural and safe method of spiritual healing
and self-improvement that everyone can use. It has been effective in
helping virtually every known illness and malady and always creates
a beneficial effect. It also works in conjunction with all other medical
or therapeutic techniques to relieve side effects and promote recovery.
So since reiki/energy work is a spiritual universal life force healing
energy there is no way it can do or cause harm even if it is intended,
reiki doesn't work that way."*
(Anonymous, 2014).

The Christian and the Muslim faiths have been known
for renouncing old pagan practices, yet it was the ancient
Celtic pagan presence I felt when I first visited Glencolmcille. This was a major step in my journey to faith and
it was that Celtic spirituality that helped Ireland in the
Christian world become known as "the land of saints and
scholars". While I have disagreements with many faiths,
I also have much admiration for many faiths too. As I
feel I am moving on a further spiritual path, I cannot be

thankful enough for the faith I was brought up on and the different faiths I have known throughout the years. Many Ascended Masters are worshipped by these many faiths.

Speaking personally, I have felt angered and wronged by much that has been done to me. I feel many people have been extremely unfair to me, but in the past they would have been unaware of my autism. Within me there is often a "should be" attitude and I have a long memory. Coming on this spiritual journey has helped me to explore myself and has helped me understand some of the reasons for this life's journey. Many of the pathways have been painful, but accepting that pain has its benefits in the long run.

# Spirituality and Pain

*"Spirituality is a personal relationship with the Devine. Religion is crowd control".*

(Anonymous)

*"Pain is an unpleasant sensory and emotional experience associated with actual or potential tissue damage, or described in terms of such damage."*

(http://www.iasp-pain.org/Education/Content.aspx-?ItemNumber=1698)

*"Pain is an unpleasant sensation occurring in varying degrees of severity as a consequence of injury, disease or emotional disorder".*

(http://www.thefreedictionary.com/pain)

In meditation we are often asked to open our hearts and this frequently includes allowing different feelings to pass as well as our pains. To some this could be called surrender, but in meditation it's often about connecting with one's self and not wasting energies fighting the unwanted. Sometimes the ability to live in the moment is a skill that needs to be learned. While being in the moment can have its pains, it also gives us the opportunity to hear and focus on sounds often much overlooked. As we grow into adulthood we learn to tolerate pain and we learn to keep our vulnerabilities enclosed. Babies and young children have often less difficulty expressing emotions and pain, but can share their laughters and joys in almost the same instant. As we mature we seek the pleasures but avoid the pains, for as we mature we strive to become socially acceptable beings. There are many forms of pain, be it physical, emotional or spiritual. Pain can affect individuals in different ways, and pain affects almost every individual. Perhaps the biggest pain for many is the inability to avoid pain, often never gaining pleasure.

There are many reasons for avoiding pain, as pain can have severe impact on our bodies. For many, growing up and being reminded of facing the pain of burning Hell when you die was not only a painful reminder, but this made many deny God's existence. . Avoiding our pain can lead others to enforce it and this can often escalate our pains. An example of this is where a politician or business leader refuses to accept responsibility for something that has gone wrong, resulting in only further questioning and often more exposure. In a world which adores celebrities and beauty, many individuals feel the unnecessary pains of ugliness when comparing themselves with airbrushed celebrities. Many of these celebrities will try to censor any undesirable images of themselves, but these unwanted images are often in greater demand by the public. In some ways I am little different as I wanted no one to know about my early childhood and early teenage years. Yet now accepting what happened in my younger years was part of the acceptance of being autistic. I also felt telling some of my pains would help explain how I felt I was treated in certain work environments.

Having a high pain threshold applies to many autistic individuals, but the opposite can be said for other autistic individuals, many of whom have heightened senses and many are prone to allergies. Many autistic individuals find it difficult to understand or communicate their pains and irritations. Other pains experienced by autistic people include being misunderstood, loneliness, rejection, intolerance, irritability, fear, anxiety and depression. While pain can be seen as cruel, pain can also tell us when to slow down, see a doctor or remind us of greater consequences due to unnecessary risks. Working in complementary therapy has made me see how individuals can be helped to accept and confront certain physical and emotional pains. Even the medical profession has encouraged the non pharmaceutical approach as a way to manage pain. As a boy I remember having a lot of pain with toothaches and recall my mother once harshly saying "offer it up for your sins". While it's something I would never say to someone, at least it could have been seen as a way to channel the pain.

When writing "Journey to Faith", I talked about my fascination of the lives of saints as a young boy. Many saints went through great suffering, some being tortured and executed. Yet I don't remember any of them wanting revenge, retribution or blaming others for their painful and unjust situations. As a boy growing up in the 1970s, I secretly wanted to reach the level of those saints but choosing to die for my faith was not an option. Writing now, this almost makes me sound like a religious fanatic, but I was taught dying for my faith rather than changing religion would mean going to a eternal higher place.

As the 1980s progressed I moved away from religious bliss and became more involved in the secular world, with a strong desire for women. While boarding school played a role in this, I was also changing as a teenager and thinking of a future with poor job prospects. I also wanted to be more like others and not being able to get a girlfriend gave me a sense of failure. These early teenage years gave me such a sense of mental pain that I often wished I were dead. Moving to Mohill eased those certain anxieties and it was the first time in the 1980s I enjoyed being a teenager, a time which also included enjoying the music of U2, Frankie Goes to Hollywood, The Smiths and The Cure. Yet despite developing a more cheerful outlook, it did not bring me back to closeness with God. I felt enjoying life was an entitlement and this outlook would be expanded when moving to England in the mid 1980s.

When I moved to England my political outlook was more Conservative. While this may surprise some, I do not regret this part of my life. As there are good people in various religious faiths, there are also good people in nearly all political divides. For it is and will be diversity that will help change the world to be a better place.

My Conservative outlook was to soon change with increased job sackings and becoming more aware of authority and capitalist exploitation. So too were my religious views changing and by the late 1980s I saw nothing wrong with being sexually active and I considered religion to be part of the ruling establishment. By now I saw suffering in the world as unnecessary and manmade, often as a result of exploitation. I also began to think "how dare religious establishments consider socialism to be evil, when all they are doing are fighting for basic rights?"

In the nineteenth century many were outraged to hear the likes of Marxists saying "people will turn away from religion". Yet writing in the twenty-first century there's a continuing decline in church attendance and religion in Britain and Ireland. One prediction where Karl Marx was probably right was that working conditions would continue to get worse. Where I feel Marx was misguided was considering all workers would realize the source of their pain and overthrow the ruling class.

From my own viewpoint there are many reasons why this has not happened. Many do not blame the capitalist ruling class for the pains in this world, while for others there are their own personal pains and too many distractions to allow them to think of politics. The many distractions include entertainment like reality TV, music shows, individuals' own personal pain and grief, and for many there is the feeling "I'm all right, Jack".

Some would say that "many people are burying their heads in sand", or living in denial. The fact is we live in a world where it is getting easier to "numb" our pains. We are living in more advancing times with increasing treatments for different illness and many have wanted to know, can there be a treatment or cure for autism? Personally speaking "I don't think so", but I do feel acceptance can go a long way in the advancement and progress of many autistic individuals.

Acceptance is needed not only by the individual, but also by family, loved ones and relevant people in that individual's life. Often the loved one of an autistic or disabled individual has difficulty accepting the news. Often it is not the disabled person or autistic person with a difference, but sometimes those loved ones who are often avoiding their own personal pains. Personal pains includes marital or relationship difficulties as well as many individuals experiencing financial, employment and work difficulties.

. As the 1980s rolled into the 1990s and my love life became more painful, I channelled much of my pain into more positive means like Socialist politics. However, I also numbed my pains with alcohol, drugs and having a good time. As a socialist I also came to believe in equal opportunities and that everyone should be entitled to the world's luxuries.

At this time I felt the concept of pain and suffering was something encouraged by the religious and ruling establishment to make individuals submissive and accept the status quo. I was now becoming more aware of being depressed, being a first year student nurse. While I was aware of being stressed and depressed in the past, this time I decided to do something about it. I decided to see a counsellor as I was not going to let the pains of my love life stop me being a student nurse.

Over the next few years I met my future wife, Helen, became a mental health nurse and got married. In addition I found God again in my life, but in a different manner from when I was a boy. Depression turned more to anxiety, even though anxiety had been ruling me throughout my life. I also had time off work with chest pains and low mood, but one thing I could not accept was my poor communication. So moving to a different area to avoid criticism of my poor communication was not the most difficult of decisions.

Soon I would learn there would be continuing "pain-in-the-arse managers" and difficulty in my communication continued to be a concern. Eventually I would be assessed as being autistic, which I see not as a cross or a suffering, but a wonderful relief. I felt receiving this news could not have come at a better time in my life as I am not sure how I would have responded to the same news twenty years before. Over the last four years I have felt being autistic as less of a disability, but more of a gift. Where I felt it was a disability was with certain employers, when I failed to meet their expectations. While expectations are different for many, sometimes the problem lies not only in the employer's expectations, but also in the employee's fears.

As the years have moved on I have come to see "my weakness" as part of my identity. Many other people may find that a pain as we live in a world which practically tells us "second best is just a mess". More recently I discovered I had tinnitus and while it was annoying at first, I quickly decided to live with it and it no longer bothers me. Over the years I have learned to accept rather than fight physical, emotional or spiritual pain; this allows for moving forward.

Suffering is not pleasant for anyone, but there is the expression "no pain, no gain". Certainly the rise of tattoo studios has shown many people are not scared of pain, which perhaps explains why I have no tattoos.

Working in mental health I got to know many women who self-harmed, mainly by cutting themselves. I remember one woman saying that cutting herself eased her mental anguish. As regards avoiding pain Kirkel (2012) states the following:

*"Avoiding pain holds it in place. In other words what resists, persists. The pain might persist in a different form. It might go into our bodies and persist as un-wellness or disease. It might persist as depression. It might persist as some kind of avoidance behaviour, what we usually refer to as addiction.*

(Kirkel, M., 2012, p.201).

Part of pain can include feelings and emotions and when working therapeutically with individuals in assertiveness, avoiding feelings was not encouraged. While making individuals aware of their different feelings, it became important not to label them as "good" or "bad". What was important was the ability for them to communicate how someone felt about a situation. Personally I have felt that in order for someone to communicate their feelings to someone, they first must accept and communicate those feelings with themselves. However, communicating those feelings of pain can often be more difficult.

There is the view that the "challenges we face are what has made us the wonderful people we are". Sometimes it's easy to feel guilty to see so much unnecessary suffering and pain in this world, especially when there's so much inequality. Yet it is difficult to judge the many rich and privileged, when many may have secret pains or are unable to have abundance in their lives. Pain for the privileged could include shame, intolerance, insecurity, fear, being misunderstood and many pains similar to the those of the rest of the population. Many would say one of the biggest pains and fears for the rich and privileged would be "loss of wealth".

As an autistic individual I have became attached to certain items or people that without which I would have felt lost. Losses in my life have included jobs, certain possessions, places I've lived, lifestyles, work colleagues and girlfriends. There have been many other losses in my life, but some of the losses mentioned above could have been due to forming unnecessary attachments?

*"You only loose what you cling to"*
(Buddha)

Some people consider pain and suffering can bring us closer to God, but I believe there are other means of getting closer to God. I feel it inappropriate to judge those who always numb their pain; especially when we never lived in their pain.

I know accepting certain pains can never be easy, but overcoming certain fears may lead to many individuals learning more about themselves and therefore having a more enriching life. To me, having an enriching life is about looking at spirituality and where God fits in.

Spirituality is more than religion, as it looks at our relationship with both our internal and our external world. Spirituality also looks beyond our identity and our meaning of life. Perhaps the biggest pain for spirituality is often the bad reputation it has been given, and spirituality is not short of its critics. In science and health, spirituality is seen as lacking research and evidence. Many religions see, spirituality encouraging people to find their own meaning of life, which might not necessarily include God.

Spirituality has helped me find peace, love and joy in my life. Spirituality has helped me accept many life pains and anxieties, as I have explored in this chapter.

### Reference

Kirkel, M. (2012) *Mary Magdalene Beckons*, Into the Heart Creations, Santa FE, New Mexico.

# Changes

Changes occur in everyone's life. Some changes are forced, some changes we have to make and some changes we make are part of our control. As parents we make changes for our children's benefit and changes are made for individuals unable to make certain decisions. Changes are something that occurred often in my lifetime and not all were in my control. Changes in my outlook have been important, as I feel writing about myself twenty years ago would have sounded different. As an autistic individual even the changes for the best and changes within my control were exhausting and anxious moments of my life.

Changes are something I experienced from my earliest memory and one of my earliest memories of change was when the family moved from London to Luton. While memories get distorted I remember liking the move to Luton, as Luton seemed smaller and quieter than London. My next memory of change was when the family had to move to a relative's house after my first visit to Ireland. I remember not enjoying the stay, but felt a great relief when the family moved into a new house. It was like our family were together again and it was shortly after this I started school in St Margaret's, Farley Hill, Luton.

Moving to Ireland was a difficult change and that was

part due to expectations. Moving to the countryside was a disappointment, when I hoped we would live in Dublin. Looking back now that would have been unrealistic as my father had already found work in Longford, as soon as we arrived in Ireland. That would be considered a miracle these days, looking at the current economic climate of the twenty-first century.

After living with the grannies for a few months in 1972, we moved into our new house. We had viewed the house before the move and I found myself looking forward to living in it. I then remember being shown Rossan School and this was a culture shock compared with the modern primary school I attended in Luton.

I remember the first day, walking to the school and there were quite a few welcoming neighbours and kids. While it was a school of unfamiliar faces, I remember one particular neighbour coming into the classroom. This was a relief seeing a familiar face from attendance at Aughavas church. Break-times became traumatic, as I found certain kids rough and wanting to fight. In addition it was the first time I experienced the cane used as corporal punishment. Having been used to previously travelling home from school by bus, walking home did not seem to bother me.

Over the weeks I found the relief teacher strict but fair and I guess it was that she was an old teacher. A new permanent teacher named Mrs Kavanagh came into post and she was a wonderful teacher. So much so, that even now if I heard she was teaching one of my kids, I would feel "they are in safe hands". Over the weeks I found the older school pupils caring and as for the younger rougher pupils, I think that was their survival method. Yet more changes were to take place later in the year, when my mother was in hospital for a few weeks. This was a challenging time and I remember sharing this in a conversation with my grandmother, as an adult many years later. I remember saying to my grandmother,

"Back then it was not that I wanted no grannies around. I just wanted my mother at home."

I remember feeling the relief of my mother returning home with a new baby, but I recall little after that. I do fondly remember First Holy Communion preparations with Mrs Kavanagh and she never used the cane. Soon further changes were to take place moving to the Master's room, where the cane was used frequently by Mr Donavan. Complaining about being caned made someone look a wimp. If my parents knew I was caned, it would only lead to further punishments.

The few years of caning came to an end with moving to secondary school. Looking back now, the kids at Rossan accepted my strange behaviours. However, at secondary school I seemed to be a source of entertainment to certain pupils. The secondary school years were a challenge which saw a number of changes. Yet one change that was for the better was my move to Marian College Mohill in 1983.

The last three years in Ireland were perhaps the happiest years of my life, until moving to England in 1986. Luton was a suitable move with members of my family and the presence of an Irish community, but it was not the Luton from my childhood.

Luton brought more changes than I'd anticipated and I found even the Luton-born of Irish parentage were different from me. As someone who was part of the community of Aughavas and Mohill, I saw Luton as having different nationalities living and socializing as different communities. Among other changes I found that Luton was not as tolerant as I'd expected and I experienced changes regarding employment. Still, being in Luton motivated changes to my education and by 1992 I had achieved a HND in Public

Administration. This, sadly, was followed by not being allowed a grant to complete my degree. Other changes followed, including unemployment, as well as going from being a respected care worker to a low paid pot washer. As well as experiencing relationships breaking up, I would experience changes in employment situations, changes in living locations and changes in standards of livings.

Changes have been something that has affected much of my life, and while many changes were painful, some resulted in pleasure. Many changes have given me deep anxiety, increased depression and have dented my self-esteem. Yet there have also been occasions when if I had not made certain changes, my life would have been a greater despair.

# Glasgow Celtic

It is said you should never discuss in a public house football, politics and religion, the main reasons being due to
fights and arguments, as well as there often being high
tensions with heavy alcohol consumption. Many have felt
they have been better able to discuss politics and religion
in a public house, rather than a place of worship or a
political institution. Some may be surprised to know that I
don't like offending other people and I have worked hard
to respect the different opinions of others, despite having
a different outlook. I remember selling copies of Socialist Worker newspaper when I was living in Luton. I also
remember being worried not to offend family and relatives,
which other SWP comrades did not seem to understand.
Indeed, I feel proud, over the years, to have integrated
with groups of people who believed in what they stood
for. There are certain issues I will not back down on like
equality of wealth and opportunity, free speech, freedom
of expression and sexuality, opposition to public health
and education cutbacks and opposition to war. We can all
change our outlooks as this helps in our response to situations, but what many professionals fail to understand is:

"You can't change the football club you support."

What cannot be changed for me is being autistic and

Irish. If others have a problem with that, that's their pain not mine. Being a true football supporter has its pains, as it often means supporting that club through hard times as much as good times. For me, that has being a big part of my life, being a supporter of Glasgow Celtic football club.

*"Celtic Football Club is the most successful club in the world, no one can deny that."*

(Bill Shankly – one of the greatest football managers of all time)

*"Celtic, like Barcelona, are more than a football club. Our clubs are a symbol of a culture and community that has not always been made welcome in their respective countries."*

(Xavi – Barcelona midfielder)

As a Celtic football supporter many people would expect me to say that Celtic winning the European Championship in 1967 was the greatest sporting event ever, but for me it was the success of the Leitrim Gaelic Football team of 1994. I was only a year old when Celtic won the European Championship in 1967, while in 1994 I was in my late twenties and my academic career had stalled, but Leitrim winning the Connacht championship was a big lift to my pride. Leitrim winning the Connacht Gaelic Football championship in 1994 and Glasgow Celtic winning the European football championship in 1967 had some similarities, as both teams were underdogs in major sporting competitions. For Leitrim it was 1927 when they previously won the Connacht football championship and let's hope it will not be a sixty year wait for Celtic to win another European football championship. Leitrim is a county that has seen much poverty and emigration over the last two hundred years and similarly Glasgow Celtic symbolizes vast poverty experienced by Irish immigrants coming to Glasgow in the late nineteenth and early twentieth centuries. Indeed, the many Irish in Glasgow and the many that emigrated from Leitrim would have also experienced discrimination for being Catholic.

It was this catholic awareness of Glasgow Celtic in the 1970s that made me admire the club, especially learning that Glasgow Rangers was the Protestant team. Yet at the time I was a Liverpool football supporter, but my favourite Scottish team was Celtic. As a kid growing up 1970s Ireland, it was the English football league we focused on, as it was there the talents of Irish players like Don Givens and George Best shone. Little did we know that Celtic had continued success in Europe in the early 1970s, something which was the envy of many English football clubs. Yet at the time I was a football enthusiast first, unlike Nick Hornby in his book *Fever Pitch* where he states "being an Arsenal supporter first, a football supporter second".

Football for me was a means for making use of my non imaginative play and a means of interacting with the boys at school. As prior to that school break times, meant not knowing what to do. While football is built on the structure of winners and losers, it's also where people's innate competiveness works perfectly together. Sadly innate competiveness has been incorporated into business, dividing workers, and is even used in healthcare. Some would say "football and sports is a disguise for capitalism"; I would go further to say "football and certain international sporting competitions can sometimes be a disguise for war". For example no one can forget Republic of Ireland's last World Cup qualifying game against Northern Ireland in 1993. On the other side, football and sports bring people together and in the early 1990s, football was something that gave many people in Ireland a sense of pride and hope. Football and sports are also a means of creating fit and healthy individuals, as well as burning off any excess anger. Spirituality can be felt when attending football matches, as there's often a greater sense of unity among supporters than at many church services.

As a boy in the mid 1970s I had an interest in the different football teams and the footballers who played for them. For Celtic that was Danny McGrain and Kenny Dalglish, who to this day are football greats. Recently both these players were included in the all time Celtic eleven as voted by the fans:

R. Simpson
Danny McGrain, Tommy Gemmell, Bobby Murdoch,
Billy McNeil
Bertie Auld, Jimmy Johnstone, Paul McStay, Kenny
Dalglish
Henrik Larsson, Bobby Lennox

Kenny Dalglish, signing for Liverpool from Celtic in 1977, was seen by a Liverpool supporter as the ideal replacement for Kevin Keegan, who was considered by many the greatest footballer in the world. Kenny Dalglish was to continue that role as Liverpool was probably the greatest football club in the world in the late 1970s and early 1980s, and this was when Maradona was known as the new Pelé. 1978 was a year of disappointments as I had to remain an extra year in primary school, but Liverpool did not win the league and to rub salt in the wounds Rangers won the treble in Scotland. For many there was a feeling of hating Glasgow Rangers more than loving Glasgow Celtic, which would shape my future football interests. Yet Scotland in the 1980s was to see the rise of the New Firm, with the success of Aberdeen and Dundee United in Europe. Indeed Dundee United looked like a classic European team, in their Adidas football stripe.

As the 1980s moved in my interest in both Gaelic Football and Associated Football declined and I preferred to stay at home during weekends. Often this was time spent listening to much of my favourite music. Many neighbours noted I stopped going to see Aughavas Gaelic Football team play and I remember feeling irritated with the radio and television Gaelic games commentary of Michael O'Hare. Of course this was something not to admit at the time, as it would have been seen as blasphemy growing up in Ireland. Another form of blasphemy in Ireland at that time were stating you hated the song "One Day at a Time" by Gloria. As the 1980s progressed, music became the soul of my life and my interest in football was getting to a low point. Yet as crowds seemed to be decreasing in English football, the Old Firm games of Celtic v Rangers with their large crowds were the envy of many English football clubs.

As I was moving to England in 1986, so was Rangers seeing English players move up their way. Glasgow Rangers had the spending power and soon their success would make them the pride of Britain. As well as that they would become the club many English football fans would admire and the Glasgow Rangers' influence led England football supporters to singing songs like "No Surrender". Many years later, when getting married, my wife suggested singing "Give me Joy in my Heart". I said "no" due to its being sung by England and Glasgow Rangers supporters as "No Surrender".

"No Surrender" is a slogan used by the Ulster Unionists and there is still a strong relationship between the Ulster Unionists and Glasgow Rangers. Indeed some Ulster Unionists still see Gaelic football and hurling as "Fenian" games and one Ulster Unionist politician recently complained when someone wore a Gaelic Football replica in an English soap opera. Gaelic football and hurling get no mention in the British sporting media, yet Gaelic games have become a recent new surprise to many in Britain, as they have been recently shown on Sky Sports and many are amazed at the players' ability.

*"No surprises as Gaelic games have been kept away from mainstream sport news in Britain. Yet it took many years for Gaelic games to be televised on BBC Northern Ireland and UTV."*

(Charles, 2014)

This was a view I expressed to a friend recently when watching a Glasgow Celtic game. My disgust at politics being brought into Gaelic games goes back to 1989 when Antrim reached the All Ireland Hurling final and no Ulster Unionist politician attended Croke Park. Ulster Unionist politicians have for many years enjoyed a close relationship with the British political establishment. When I moved over to England in the 1980s I had little political interest, but attitudes towards Irish were not good following the Brighton bombing. As an Irishman who experienced certain hostilities in England, I now channelled my football energies into supporting Glasgow Celtic.

While in 1987 Glasgow Rangers would win the league with its influx of English players, the following year Celtic would win the double on their centenary year and would have a few players representing Republic of Ireland in Euro 1998. Two years later an even greater Celtic significance came when Republic of Ireland qualified for their first World Cup finals and when Packie Bonner made the historic penalty save to send Republic of Ireland to the quarter finals of the 1990 World Cup. This was a time when my many friends and I would go to watch Republic of Ireland in our Celtic replicas. At this stage not only was I proud to be a Celtic supporter as an Irishman, but also as a Socialist. Yet around this time I remember being asked not to wear my Celtic top at a social occasion, because some ex-skinheads might be there. This annoyed me as football was always my love and if I had no interest in football, I would not be wearing a Glasgow Celtic football replica.

While Glasgow Rangers were giving the impression of being an open club when they signed their first Catholic and a black footballer, in reality they were still strongly linked to Unionists in Northern Ireland and also had a right wing political following. Yet while many Northern Irish Unionists were proud to be British, many people in England did not see the difference and saw them as Irish no different from nationalists. This led me to write a poem about a drinking mate of mine.

### Belfast

For the Belfast man is Irish, whatever side he's on.
No one knows the difference, when he's in other lands.
For both sides run away to much forget the past.
Belfast is in Ireland, Belfast is in Ireland.

As a Celtic supporter the progression of the 1990s became frustrating, with Rangers eventually winning nine in a row and Celtic picking up little silverware. This gave Rangers a greater presence in Europe and Rangers were in the position to speak about the foreign player rule, as part of Rangers' success was the declining number of Scottish players. Round this time I was sharing a house in London with a Glasgow Rangers supporter and while there were differences in opinions, we also had an understanding. So coming from work one evening I returned to the house saying that UEFA has listened to the concerns of Glasgow Rangers on the foreign player rule and have made some alterations:

"Glasgow Rangers will be allowed to play three non Protestant players in European games, while Glasgow Celtic will be allowed to play three non Catholics in European games."

Overall this particular Glasgow Rangers supporter was one of the best house mates I had and we both liked going for the occasional pint. To be honest I have known many good Glasgow Rangers supporters over the years, just like I have known many good people of different religious and political divides.

Despite Rangers winning nine Scottish titles, there was little to show in Europe compared with when Celtic won nine in a row more than twenty years before. This was often a major part of conversations with my Glasgow Rangers house mate. Still, in 1998 Celtic won the Scottish League, halting Rangers ten in a row. It was a day I will never forget and listening to football matches on radio always gives me deep anxiety, but that anxiety was rewarded by a wonderful relief when Harold Bratback scored the second goal for Glasgow Celtic to give them a two nil victory and the league title. It was an evening I walked round St Albans proudly in my Glasgow Celtic top and I remember many people in the pub approaching me and expressing congratulations.

As the 1990s progressed into a new millennium, Celtic's fortunes were changing and Glasgow Celtic was rising like the Irish economic Celtic Tiger. Indeed, I was living and working in Ireland when Celtic reached the Europa final in 2003 and were beaten in extra time. At this time, while I was always proud of Celtic and its Irish roots, I was equally proud of Celtic signing non Catholics for many years. Many would say "so you should be proud", after all I am in a mixed marriage and proud. However, in other chapters I discuss further the link between other faiths and spirituality. For me, watching Celtic play can be a spiritual experience, as it can sometimes bring people more together than a church service. One day I would like it if Helen came with me to watch Celtic play at Celtic Park, as I have found it a family friendly venue with a good atmosphere.

Over the years of being a Glasgow Celtic supporter I have learned Celtic is more than a football club, it's part of my identity. Over time, Celtic supporters have demanded justice for Ireland and Palestine, as well as supporting many working class struggles. This has often come at a price, with fines and sanctions imposed on Celtic and their supporters, despite being victims of sectarian attacks. I oppose all attacks, be they on people's sexual orientation, nationality or religion, and I oppose physical attacks on Glasgow Rangers supporters, who are often seen waving Israeli flags as well as Union Jack flags at football games. Yet Glasgow Celtic have many Jewish supporters and with the recent Israeli assault on Gaza, I became concerned at increasing attacks on Jewish people worldwide and I was inspired to write the following on a social networking site.

*It's sad that the ordinary people have to pay the price for political injustice. As I do not see what is happening in Gaza as a Jewish issue. Sadly history is repeating itself where religion is being used. Yet over the last 100 years wars have been a result in the fight to control wealth resources. With rising hatred perhaps the words of Jesus are still relevant "Father forgive them, for they do not know what they are doing".*
( Myself, 2014).

Sometimes telling people which club you support opens

you up to be seen as subjective, but objectively speaking everyone has an individual identity. Part of my individual identity is being a Glasgow Celtic supporter and this is something I included when giving a Spirituality presentation. At the time of compiling the Spirituality presentation, I was not fully aware of being autistic, so being autistic was not included as part of my identity. Despite making no apologies for being autistic, a big part of my identity includes my beliefs, my love for good music and good books and my love for Glasgow Celtic. Just like there are different Celtic supporters, so are there different types of autistic individuals. It was developing an identity and certain interests that enabled my motivation to learn to read.

A big part of my book reading development in the 1970's came from reading football comics like *Roy of the Rovers* and *Tiger*. It even inspired me to create my own fictional football characters, who could play good football, unlike me. As for the football comics, playing football was the characters' lives and I don't remember any experiencing being football supporters. While wanting to play football was part of my life as a boy, unlike the comic book characters, music was an even greater passion. Perhaps this is not strange for many Glasgow Celtic football supporters there is a close link with music, especially when the father of the legendary Gil Scott-Heron played for Celtic. Many other musicians, like Simple Minds and U2, are proud Celtic football supporters, while not forgetting the many other talented artists.

Loving music and football has often made me wonder, if I were twenty years older, how I would have celebrated Celtic's 1967 European championship. I think the answer would be "stoned", as there was the possibility I would have also been part of the 1967 "Summer of Love". Actually it would have been a unique experience tripping with hippy music along with a free love woman, knowing Celtic was the greatest football team and putting the world to rights with my friends. Some would say that sounds like a perfect world, but I am not sure about that. I enjoyed attending music festivals and later raves in my twenties to my early thirties. Indeed, in the 1990s when Ecstasy and dance culture were popular, it was noted in some areas there were good times between football supporters and no violence. I knew many people who, like me, loved both music and football and I remember seeing some people wearing Celtic replicas at music festivals.

Like many Celtic supporters I know what it's like being in the job hunt, where chances of getting a half decent job are as possible as Celtic winning next season's European championship. Because of the competition in the job market I have got feedback from possible employers of concerns with anxiety and travelling distance from work and being too long out of certain areas of nursing. Yet the most interesting feedback was being told I was "too qualified for the job", even though I felt it was more the job for me. Job satisfaction means more to me than money and for many years I felt compelled to remain in nursing due to financial and mortgage reasons and to remain on the nursing register. Yet it is jobs with great job satisfaction that have given me much stability in my life. Many football supporters had dreams of playing for their favourite football club, and I was no exception; and even if I had the football skills of Pelé or Messi, I would still want to play for Glasgow Celtic, but then I am a Celtic football supporter and not a football player.

# Autism can be Wonderful

I hear things more loudly
I see things more clearly
I smell things more strongly
I feel things you don't

I have autism

As many are now aware, for most of my life I was unaware I was autistic, yet the discovery that I was was such a wonderful experience and realization for me. But much of my life has been a struggling experience and I have been autistic since birth. However, discovering being autistic did not get off to the best start as I expected my management would no longer question my communication difficulties because of that being disability discrimination. How wrong I was. I guess it had come from my awareness of learning disabilities when, even as a boy, I heard of children with learning disabilities not being given corporal punishment for doing wrong, unlike the rest of us. So I guess I was expecting similar treatment and also had an awareness of disability discrimination from when I was working in Horsefield. However, I have forgiven certain managers as they may have been under pressure from the top. Autistic forgiveness can be difficult as much of what is said to us can be over internalized and letting go of negative memories can be difficult, but developing a faith and a more positive outlook has enabled forgiveness.

Having autism can be a wonderful experience and, yes, it's true that having feelings of anxiety, anger, and feeling frightened much of the time and not able to think outside the box poses many difficulties. It is not surprising that sometimes people are amazed at what we can't comprehend. I guess it's like someone who knows how the world operates but may be incapable of knowing how to put things away in their own home. Being autistic allowed me to focus to such an extent that some people would say "tripping without being drugged out". It has allowed me almost to go into trance states in worship, relaxation and listening to certain music; it has allowed me to explore interests I can really get deep into, and finally it has allowed me to focus on what I can do best. Having strong senses has also allowed me to enjoy certain images, smells, feelings and sounds.

The other unique thing for many people with Autistic Spectrum Disorder (ASD) is that they have many unusual strengths, like:

- Attention to detail and intense focus.
- Skills in particular areas.
- Many people with ASD are known for being loyal and punctual employees.
- Autistic people, like many disabled people, are loyal and try extra hard in work environments, as getting another job can be more difficult compared with non disabled people.
- While anxiety and fear can have negative effects on both physical and mental health, it has also

prevented me from taking others for granted and avoiding certain illegal risks.

- Being non judgemental.
- Many people with ASD who don't socialize much are not so much anti-social, they just have no tolerance for lies, bullshit, or as many Irish like me would say, "fake drama".
- While limited intervention has led to many people with ASD struggling, there have been many successes with people with the disorder who received appropriate support and intervention.
- While people with ASD are seen as often lacking empathy and failing to respond to others' emotions, sometimes people with ASD can be oversensitive and often will feel their pains of sensitivity. Many people with ASD are anxious not to upset or insult other people. The belief "do unto others as they would do unto you" very much applies.
- Many people with ASD may be scared of animals, like dogs, and often for good reason. Yet many with ASD love animals and relate very well to them. They would despise animal cruelty.
- Many people with ASD may be seen as indecisive, but once they make a decision there is no going back for many.
- Many people with ASD can be analytical and observant. From my experience as a student nurse, I was praised in one of my assignments for observing how student nurses were used to balance the staff numbers on clinical placements. I supported this by showing written evidence from one of the nursing magazines.
- The need for variety is seen as a human need and

many think people with ASD have limited interests. While it's true too much variety leads to confusion and being overwhelmed, it could lead to many planning certain repetitive activities. Yet many people with ASD often like to expand part of that particular interest.

- Variety is something that does not apply to many individuals with ASD, as many have a quest for knowledge and are keen to expand their interests, which may surprise many. Variety is something many High Functioning individuals with ASD need, as having a plan B can help reduce certain anxieties. For many autistics with specific skills and often limited coping mechanisms, awareness of variety of locations is useful, especially if it means having to relocate to maintain work in specific skills.

- Finding out the learning experience that can benefit an individual's behaviour. This comes from my experience where I observed a reduction in disruptive behaviour in certain individuals depending on the subject taught.

- Many people with ASD have worked hard to imitate certain role models in order to fit into society's social roles.

- From a personal opinion, having reduced anxiety means improved ability to trust, improved mood and increase in self-esteem. A decrease in anxiety can mean increased ability to concentrate on other tasks due to less distraction. Many autistic individuals can express their joys non verbally.

- Many people with ASD are not suited to jobs where there's a strong dependence on Performance Management – mental health nursing, nursing mentor, supervisor or shelf stacker in a busy crowded supermarket – but their strengths can be seen in jobs like photographer or paralegal or the many jobs where they have control and are not subject to too much management pressure or being put on the spot. See also the article by Temple Grandin (1999): http://www.iidc.indiana.edu/?pageId=596.

- Many people with ASD rarely lie and from my own experience I get really annoyed when being put under pressure to lie. Actually, I have always found it easier to tell the truth and find having to tell lies a deep anxiety. For myself, I dislike lies told by media and I often like to research the facts.
- Body language is a mysterious, unspoken way in which people unconsciously communicate what is really on their minds. It has been noted that my opinion or disapproval of something will often be communicated without a word being said.
- While many people with ASD have difficulty with remembering and memory, exceptionally good memory is also part of being autistic. I have quite a strong memory of my early childhood years and I now find myself remembering folks from school many other family members have forgotten.

Other strengths were found in a useful website: http://www.yourlittleprofessor.com/benefits.html

They included :

- Strong conceptualization skill – Able to mentally model complex systems, may develop instinctive understanding of the system from this internalized model);
- Attention to detail (can identify inconsistencies in processes or communications);
- Honest, straightforward (can treat people fairly);

- Intense focus.

Other strengths include:
- People with ASD live in the moment. Many people with ASD find mindfulness meditation useful.
- Many people with ASD rarely judge others, as many observe differently compared with neurotypical people.
- Autistic people are passionate and take a deep interest in certain subjects. Many people with ASD often get grief about their unusual subject interests, but speaking personally, "it would be a more cut throat world if everyone had the same interests".
- People with ASD are not tied to social expectations, even though from experience I was expected to comply with many social expectations.
- People with ASD have fantastic memories, and from my own experience I have early childhood memories of being in London in the 1960s. I still have memories of certain events over thirty years ago as if they were yesterday. While forgiveness has not been easy regarding certain situations, having a long memory has also allowed me to remember friends and those who were good to me.
- People with ASD play fewer mind games and they assume that you won't play them either. Indeed, many autistic individuals have been victims of bullying, which has also included mind games. Certainly, working in mental health had its difficulties dealing with individuals with personality disorders, often playing mind games on occasions.
- People with ASD have fewer hidden agendas. Part of this includes certain autistic individuals, includ-

ing myself, having been known for saying what's on their mind, often to the embarrassment of others.
- People with ASD have many strengths and skills that can be of benefit for many neurotypicals.
- People with ASD are also known for independent thinking. Often this results in novel "big picture" insights due to different ways of looking at things, ideas, and concepts.

Although some areas of development are delayed in a child with autism, these children often exhibit skills beyond their years in other areas. These intellectual strengths may overshadow the developmental problems experienced by a child.

Prior to my awareness of being autistic I did not like my vulnerabilities exposed and I think that applies to many neurotypical people too. As autistic people have many vulnerabilities I don't care for workplace managers' excuses when they push employees' vulnerable buttons, even when under orders. It can never be acceptable and I feel it is a form of abuse.

Describing myself in the third person can be difficult as it means thinking outside the box. It takes much focus to refer to myself in the third person, but it's even more difficult for other people affected by autism and this is often accompanied by other issues. For me and many who have autism, we often live in our own world, a world much misunderstood by many.

Despite being autistic I have shared many similarities with neurotypicals, for instance having intimate relationships, one night stands, working most of my life, abusing drugs and alcohol and even breaking rules at school and work. Other similarities include a career in nursing, teaching, care work and catering, while extra-work activities included being a union representative, political activist and volunteer youth worker. Indeed the autistic community needs more political activists and someone with more guts than me. Perhaps I share one of the greatest satisfactions, and that is getting married. Although low mood, depression and anxiety have played major roles in my life, I have also experienced the many joys of living.

While there are many misunderstandings about autism, I still think people who are autistic have much to teach the world. I say that because as a mental health nurse for many years, I learnt much from people experiencing difficulties with mental health issues. As someone with autism I was able to do a presentation on autism awareness to one of the care homes in Horsefield. While I was able to explain the difficulties in autism and my own experience, there were other autistic personal difficulties that I did not include in the original presentation. Yet while I was compiling the presentation I needed time to concentrate and also needed time to focus, which is important for people like me.

I feel autistic people need to be allowed to focus even to the point that other tasks may need to be overlooked, and some may call that a form of obsession. Yet that focus is needed for concentrating and if that focus is broken or distracted, it's like breaking something valuable which cannot be repaired. While obsession concerns many, without obsessions, focus and addictions to certain projects and topics of interest, certain achievements in this world may have never existed. I too have needed certain addictive traits to get motivated. While some people are addicted to drugs, leading to negative consequences, others can be addicted to money, but that addiction seems to have benefited the establishment. Indeed the media has become aware of what attracts some people's focus easily, like television soap operas and the reality shows of the twenty-first century. Keeping on the topic of focus, many autistic people will get angry when their focus is distracted or broken, just as many others will get angry when a certain object is broken. However, for people like me, being distracted can have severe consequences, especially when often being forgetful has been a major difficulty in my life, but this is part of the many difficulties faced in autism. In addition difficulties like being unable to remember and anger can be due to difficulty getting a proper nights sleep, which affects many autistic individuals.

Other difficulties:

- Not letting go of past events – For me this has meant remembering certain negative past events as if they were today.
- Holding grudges – This is also due to the fact that it has often taken many years to understand the reasons for certain decisions or actions.
- Difficulty taking in information – Which often contributes to communication difficulties and misunderstandings with other people.
- Difficulty often in understanding what's said.
- Misinterpreting what's said – This even gets more difficult when stressed or anxious.
- Sometimes making decisions without much thought.
- Losing my temper.
- Low tolerance.
- Mistrusting.
- Communicating.
- Difficulty forgiving even though I have wanted to forgive.
- Anger – Something I am trying to move away from

is focusing on "should be"; past mistakes, past misfortunes and those who wronged me will make me feel angry.

- Difficulty in accepting criticism and/or being corrected – Yet from my own experience, this can be due to making many errors and having the experience of constant criticism. Autistic people need much reassurance in many atmospheres of constant criticism. This is why I feel criticism must be delivered to someone who is autistic in a skilful manner as I have encountered situations where criticism was delivered appropriately and other situations where it could have been seen as more like abuse. My difficulty in accepting has also meant difficulty of being rejected by women as well as difficulty accepting that certain girls disliked me when I was a boy.

- Strongly liking, or strongly disliking, certain things, for example, certain foods – This is often due to many autistic people having strong senses that make accepting the taste of certain foods difficult. Yet as autistic I am proud of my selected likes and interests.

- Many people with Autistic Spectrum Disorder have to study how other people interact and function, which means having to double work and explains why many may get over tired.

- Many people with Autistic Spectrum Disorder find it difficult to interact in groups of people. My own experience is that I found it difficult to bring girlfriends to certain events. Often I would feel very uncomfortable when other men would engage my girlfriend in their conversation; the list could go on.

I felt more comfortable dating girlfriends in venues where it would just us two without the distraction of friends. I would have felt less anxious, as I would often not know how to behave among my friends when the current girlfriend was present.

- Excessive talking – In my experience I have found certain interests will often overtake my life and I may go on talking on that one topic being unaware of lack of interest from others.

- Difficulty in correcting someone else for mistakes without appearing to be insensitive or harsh – While working as a nursing mentor, this happened on occasions, but then I found being a nursing mentor stressful and felt I was being watched.

- Sometimes appearing shy and withdrawn, but willing to speak when spoken to, and this has often led to much misunderstanding about autistic people and is why people are reluctant to interact with them.

- Clumsiness and balance difficulties – This is why many find sport difficult. Achieving in sport was important where I grew up in Ireland and often I felt many disappointments in not achieving in sport.

- Great concern about personal working area, which has caused disagreements with family. I often wish I had more home space to do office work and work in complementary therapies.

- Problems addressing others due to issues with trust – This is often due to many people who are autistic being victims of bullying. Because of my own experiences in the past it will take me a long time to trust, especially with the way I had to leave Horsefield.

- Intense concern for privacy – While I like the company of people, many who are autistic find being in crowds very stressful. I remember when I was in boarding school, certain guys found it amusing to follow me around when I wanted to be on my own.

- Difficultly in distinguishing intimate relationships from friendships – I have experienced some regrettable fall-outs with some women where I was not sure if our friendship was intimate or not, often due to misunderstandings on my part. This is often what makes being a teenager difficult and even for High Functioning Autistic teenagers their social learning experiences may last till adulthood.

- Having to write lists to stay on schedule when things get hectic – While many may find this strange, having a list and a schedule is something that prevents increased anxiety for many autistic people.

- Very weird sense of humour, sometimes not found very humorous by others – Many who are autistic have a sense of humour, but sometimes there can be a lack of awareness of how others will respond.

- Uneasiness with completing a project for fear of failure, but often this is due to many unnecessary distractions, which make it difficult to focus on the project.

- Difficulty starting projects – From my own experience this is often due to difficulty in imagination and difficulty motivating myself.

- Interrupting in the middle of a conversation, which has been an embarrassment for my wife on occasions.

- Repetitive behaviours, and if the step-by-step scheduled routine is interrupted it causes confusion and sometimes anger – This is very important for working with autistic people and I feel is important when accepting values. Causing unnecessary inter-ruptions seems to me nothing short of bullying.

- Certain preferences in personal items, such as always picking the same clothes in stores when making a new purchase, using the same blanket, not wanting to throw away a particular pair of shoes.

- Raising of voice during stressful and frustrating sit-uations, as well as being verbally blunt.

- Difficulty hiding true emotions such as anger and sadness and being quick tempered. Although that could be also be seen as the honest side of many people with Autistic Spectrum Disorder.

- Many people with Autistic Spectrum Disorder experience difficulty in sleeping. This is some-thing I experienced for much of my life, leading to increased tiredness, decreased concentration and difficulty performing daily tasks. Over the years increase in anxiety and depression has contributed to difficulty in sleeping.

- Lacking the ability to relax away from activities, which is why many people who are autistic find time away from work difficult, especially where work may have some structure.

- Little interest in tasks that don't draw personal interest – Perhaps this could be helped by looking at areas of certain tasks that might draw interest or looking at certain tasks that could be incorporated into certain uninteresting activities.

- Having a different way of playing games with others, and this is sometimes taken the wrong way – This is often where children may find play time difficult at schools and it adds to difficulties with interacting and making friends with other kids.

- Fixating on really bad or really good experiences, as many people who are autistic see much around them in black and white.
- Limiting oneself with pursued interests without thinking of other things that can be explored.
- Confusion during stress has been something that has plagued much of my life and it is helpful for many who are autistic to get to know some of their stress causes.
- Strong sensitivity to sound, light, some tastes, odours and colours – As a kid I found certain people's odour offensive, due to poor hygiene, and I still find certain foods that would make me ill if I tried to eat them.
- Difficulty expressing emotion.
- A need for finishing one task before starting another – From my work experience there are often pressures to do other tasks and this can lead to great anxiety.
- Constantly asking questions – Yet the ability to ask certain questions can be useful. Like who would have the guts to ask "why do people vote for cruel politicians?"?
- Mental shut-down or total burst of anger when "pinned in the corner" and often viewed as vulnerable by not responding when being harassed by classmates or co-workers.
- Very easily distracted and self-injuring behaviours – Which is why focus for autistic individuals needs to be respected and distraction from focus can sometimes lead to self-injuring behaviours.
- Difficulty in starting or changing conversations – Even many High Functioning Autistic individuals have difficulty knowing when to end conversations.

- Thinking on a "one track mind" type basis and difficulty with negotiation.
- Many autistic individuals experience a wide range of mental health issues, but a recent study has raised concerns about the number of mothers of autistic individuals experiencing mental health issues.
- As autistic, my personal history, desires and fears have played a big part in how I filter communication. This filtering includes bending, which means distorting an incoming message, and patterning, which means altering the message to fit what we believe. For me, I also feel this can be due to limited imagination and difficulty absorbing information.

I was fortunate to have good parents who taught me the importance of discipline and the teachings of the Catholic Church, which influenced my outlook in both positive and negative ways. Primary school in Ireland was difficult but I was taught good Christian values and most of all I was taught how to read and write. My parents played an educational role too, but there were times I felt more like another member of a farming family, where work had to be done and if you did not work hard enough at school you would have a future of shit jobs or, worse, unemployment. While there were various difficulties my parents faced bringing up a family of seven children, and with an uncertain economic future, my parents never forced me to leave school and supported me in decisions I made in my education. I know if they had been aware I was autistic my father would have paid to send me to an appropriate school if required. In defence of my parents, it was not their fault for failing to notice my autism and like in any family there were occasional misunderstandings between other family members and myself.

Alice Hewitt, in 2014, http://disabilityintersections. com/2014/02/underlying-problem-with-autism-frame/ states that research has indicated that many children from poor working class backgrounds and children from ethnic backgrounds are not assessed early enough as being autistic. I worked for many years in both mental health and learning disabilities care and many top professionals failed to notice my autism; it was only in recent years certain people did recognize it. For me, recognizing my autism has also meant recognizing much of my true self.

As someone autistic I have needed influential people around me, like my brother, who introduced me to much good music and sensible politics. This led to remarks of "trying to be like certain people" and being seen as in my brother's shadow. While our music and politics were similar I ended up joining the SWP whereas my brother was more anarchic, and in later life when we both got into dance music, I went more into Trance music. This is why I am thankful to my parents for bringing me up in a religious faith, and even though I went on a slightly different spiritual route, my parents planted that invaluable spiritual seed. Being raised up in a religious faith, helped in my awareness of the injustice and inequality in this world. Indeed, it was my wife who introduced me to both spirituality and complementary therapies. Yet on many occasions we have gone on different spiritual paths and more recently there are even differences in our complementary therapy directions. As someone autistic I often feel I lack many imagination, but I also feel good influential people and good support networks can help in my creativity.

As autistic and proud, I still think much more can be done for autistic adults, even the High Functioning Autistics. Even for myself, if I had been diagnosed earlier, I would have found a more appropriate career and not had certain misunderstandings and fall-outs with certain people. I also consider myself lucky for having not only my direct family, but also the extended family and good friends. As for jobs, while some have been a struggle, for the majority I have had positive feedback and I am grateful for the support of management and many working colleagues over the years.

Some would say "why do you need the extra support?" and I would say "there are many areas I struggled in not only in my career, but also in my personal life and leaving Horsefield has been a major challenge". In addition there are many autistic victims of unemployment, crime, dysfunctional families and many are regular visitors to the prison system. I feel very concerned for many individuals who are seen as High Functioning Autistics, as, like many autistic individuals, some of their needs may be as great as those with special needs, and they need much care and support. In recent years I have seen good work done with many young autistic people, especially children.

The autistic children are the adults of the future and I believe there's a need for more funding to keep up the good work, as much of the work requires one to one intervention. As a young day care worker in learning disabilities I remember thinking the Social Skills and Makaton Communication training could have been more useful when these adults were younger. Sadly that service was scrapped a few years later, but that passion for young people with learning disabilities never disappeared. If governments, local governments or charities were to choose support for autistic adults or autistic children, I would say "prioritize the young first". Even though many autistic adults have been overlooked by services and have experienced mistreatment, it is something I feel the younger autistic generation should not experience. As anyone knows who has worked with autistic individuals, each has an individual identity and I believe "that's why the future autistic generation will have much to contribute to future society".

Other difficulties that accompany autism include:

- OCD (Obsessive–Compulsive Disorder)
- Learning disabilities
- ADHD (Attention Deficit Hyperactivity Disorder)
- Anxiety
- Tourette's Syndrome
- Developmental Co-ordination Disorder
- Auditory Processing and Depression (these in particular have played a big part in my struggles).

I recently learnt many people who are autistic suffer from depression and anxiety and some further concerns are highlighted in: http://www.infobarrel.com/22_Habits_of_Unhappy_People which included:

- Chronic complaining
- Retail therapy
- Binge drinking – Some may turn to drug taking or other comfort issues like comfort eating
- Worrying about the future
- Lack of hobbies – For autistic individuals this can be a concern as they might lose interest in their hobbies when low and have limited imagination to engage in other hobbies
- Eating poorly – Obesity has been a noted problem for some autistic people
- Talking poorly of others
- Holding grudges – Which has affected me
- Not having a goal
- Stopping learning
- Job hating – Which I have experienced with certain jobs

- Loneliness – Which many may be surprised to learn is experienced by many autistic individuals
- Letting negative thoughts enter your mind – Being autistic often means difficulty getting rid of negative thoughts
- Jumping to conclusions – For many who are autistic this can also be due to impairment in imagination
- Self labelling
- Worrying what others think – This has been something that has given me much anxiety throughout my life
- Letting strangers affect one's mood
- Wanting more money – Even though I feel much of the world population wants more money.

We live in a world which expects much conforming to rules. We live in a world that shows little tolerance to norms being broken, even the norms of the now glamour media. We also live in a world that wants heroes – those who fight against the odds, individuality and flexibility – but that too must conform to the rules of a world that shows little tolerance.

These days many are amazed when they see the increasing presence of people with mental and physical disabilities and even mental health issues, often making significant contributions to society. Within many people's living memory, the mentally ill and those with mental and physical disabilities, as well as women seen as sexually inappropriate, were locked away in institutions. Many will be surprised to know that the rise of institutions came with the rise of the industrial revolution. Whereas prior to the industrial revolution many people with disabilities lived in the family unit, with the rise of the industrial revolution, they had little to contribute to this progress. Some would say little has changed, with capitalism moving from industry to services provision, which often demands further progress and which has often alienated many autistic people, who may have had a routine working in factories. My years in nursing often demanded progress and quality in the profession, which often alienated certain nurses who were more hands on. Some would say they are no longer training nurses but training student nurses to become managers and nurse consultants.

This could be seen by some as an unfair attack on the nursing profession, when it gave me decent employment for more than ten years. As someone autistic perhaps I entered the wrong profession, but it did contribute to my skills as a carer in my last two years in Horsefield working in learning disabilities. However, over the years I have known many good carers and potential good nurses who have been turned down as student nurses due to developments in nursing education standards. Despite that, the last thirty years have seen progress in disability discrimination and now as it's unacceptable to remove someone from their wheelchair, exposing their vulnerabilities, so in the future I think it will be unacceptable to expose autistic people to their vulnerabilities. I feel that although in recent times gay discrimination has decreased it has still some way to go, and over the years issues like menstruation, incontinence and bladder weakness in women have become less of a taboo. Recently John Bird went a step further when writing in the *Big Issue* on the myth of the good old days:

*"There was so much that was loathsome about the 1950's, 60's and 70's and we are well out of those times. I remember how acceptable it was to talk about disabled people as 'spastics', as failed and cast-off people who were good to joke at. Women and girls were described*

*without personality, purposelessness other than to be on your arm or in your bed or up against a wall.*

*Many people looked upon foreigners as some low form of life, not just because of their colour but their culture, their food and their clothing. 'John Foreigner' was how posh people described anyone who wasn't British".*

(Bird, J., 2014, p.13)

Growing up in Ireland I remember many people thinking Protestants living in the Republic of Ireland were not proper Irish and I remember getting verbally abused for being allegedly gay. I also remember the word 'spastic' used, but it was shortened to 'spa'. Over the years improved autism awareness has come from people who are autistic themselves and I feel this progress can further continue. Of course, this progress would not have been possible without good professional support and care from the general public. For myself, I am forever grateful for the support my manager Marian gave me, as well as the staff in learning disabilities I worked with in Horsefield. Many people will question "why make public amenities and workplaces autistic friendly?" One answer could be "why is the natural countryside destroyed with roads and cities?" If humans were fast enough they would not need roads designed for fast cars and lorries. At present many countries have had to adapt health services to an increasing elderly population, yet many elderly are still making contributions to society. Autistic diagnosis looks to be on the increase and so services will need to be more autistic friendly, yet many autistic individuals have already made valuable contributions to society and can further do more in the future. I believe the future is bright, the future is autistic.

While I am no expert on autism, there are a number of suggestions I feel could benefit autistic individuals:

- Finding out what works and what does not work for them – This includes High Functioning Autistics and Savants. Yet not all Savants are autistics.
- Finding out what support family and carers need – As someone who worked as a mental health nurse for many years, I felt the strain on my own mental health after ten years. I have always felt a concern for family and unpaid carers and my wife has had no support as an informal carer, despite struggles with her physical health.
- Finding out the physical health needs of some autistic individuals, as sometimes these physical health concerns can be an indicator of whether individuals possibly have Autistic Spectrum Disorder.
- Finding out their strengths, needs and weakness.
- Finding out what motivates them.
- Finding out what creates anxiety for autistic individuals, as well as what escalates their anxiety on occasions.
- Finding out the support certain High Functioning Autistics and some Savants (like Sheldon in the TV comedy "Big Bang Theory") need who are involved in forms of freelance work or projects.
- Finding out individuals' levels of social skills and assessing appropriately in order to implement appropriate interventions. This is also relevant for autistic people who are seen as High Functioning.
- Finding out what helps in their relaxation process.
- Finding out what opportunities autistic individuals have for "me time" – This could include coming into work extra early or arising from bed an hour earlier when the workplace or the house is quiet.
- Finding out their likes and dislikes, as well as interests and possible hobbies – One of the future

approaches to autism is not overloading with choice. Malcolm Gladwell in his book *Blink* noted from experiments that limiting product choice created more sales.

- Finding out what can give them focus, depending on the individual.
- Finding out what can give them reassurance.
- Finding out, if possible, ways they can channel their anger.
- Finding out their potential stressors and sources of irritation.
- Finding out whether an individual's modality is Visual, Auditory or Kinaesthetic, also described as visual or auditory thinkers. This would be useful in deciding the types of gifts to buy, but also useful when assessing types of suitable relaxation.
- Finding out what colours are appropriate to the needs of certain autistic individuals.

http://www.iidc.indiana.edu/?pageId=596

# What's Next

Many reading my book may think I am very bitter, especially in the way I have recorded some events in my past. My answer to that is "you are free to your opinions", but I will not deny feeling very hurt regarding certain events in my life. Dealing with the past has been something difficult for me and many would say "life is tough". Many would be in denial about the hard times and various recessions in Ireland; some may say it was true, as there never were the boom times prior to the economic recessions.

I have recorded many of my life events as I experienced them and one fact is "I have forgiven many who hurt me, despite its difficulties". In reality there were many more hurtful events and traumas I chose not to write about. Even the recorded events have many changed names. There's much I feel grateful for and growing up in Ireland is certainly one treasure.

I believe being autistic means learning almost every day. I have heard stories of people having bad accidents and having to learn the basics like walking and eating again. From my own experience it is a surprise what I am still learning, as to many it is something I should have known for a lifetime.

As someone autistic, my outlook and interests are different from many people's, which has seen me at odds with many people over the years. Autistic or not we live in a world that relies more on conformity than diverting from the norm. Non conformity and creativity have been the story of people like Jesus and Vincent van Gogh, who were not held in high regard by the establishments of the time. Non conformity and creativity have been needed to challenge the many injustices in history and allow the many freedoms we take for granted. Non conformity and creativity were needed for the rise of modern popular music and the punk scene of the 1970s. So someone's strange interests of today might be everyone's craze and trend in the future.

This book started off as a part therapeutic experience for me and also an opportunity to share many misunderstandings. Over time I felt there were other experiences that needed to be shared. As I researched more I discovered how much this book may be able to help others. These others include families with autistic children, and adults struggling wondering "why they can't cope", which is why I presented a "picture" of autism within the book. While I had considered book writing before, after being made aware of being possibly autistic, I felt this was the book within me.

*"Attacking people with disabilities is the lowest form of power I can think off"*
(Morgan Freeman).

Lightning Source UK Ltd.
Milton Keynes UK
UKOW04f1502150615

253525UK00002B/17/P